MENTORING
TROUBLED YOUTH

DR. JOANNE SPENCE

GlobalEdAdvance
Press

MENTORING TROUBLED YOUTH

Copyright © 2011 / 2013 by Joanne Spence

Library of Congress Control Number: 2011938655

Spence, Joanne, 1959

Mentoring Troubled Youth ISBN 978-1-935434-61-0

Subject Codes and Description:

    1: EDU 045000: Education: Counseling-Crisis Management 2: REL 091000
    Religion: Education –Children & Youth 3: BUS 106000: Business & Economics:
    Mentoring and Coaching.

Cover design by Brian Lane Green

Printed in the USA

GlobalEdAdvance Press
www.gea-books.com

Acknowledgement

To all the participants of this research, a heartfelt thanks to you. The data in this book would not be possible without you. For those who were in unusual circumstance, I pray that this book will stimulate the minds of the policy makers so that appropriate intervention would be taken to assist in alleviating your situation.

To all the youths who participated in this study, your dreams are just a hand reach away from you. Stretch your hands, exercise you faith and reach for your goals, because your destiny depends on it.

To all my clients throughout my profession who allowed me to be the sounding board to the issues they faced, your experiences have provided me with invaluable knowledge that I hope will be used to create a more lucrative environment for you. I am also grateful to the reviewer, Dr. Daphne Phillip.

To my three children who provided insight on youth issues and who allowed me to gain firsthand experience of raising young men and women. Thank you for making parenting an easy task.

Contents

Gen. Powell shaking hands with Dr. Joanne Spence on his arrival in Trinidad to launch the National Mentorship Program.

PROLOGUE

General Colin L. Powell, USA (Ret.)

Words to Digest

The less you associate with some people, the more your life will improve. Anytime you tolerate mediocrity in others, it increases your mediocrity. An important attribute in successful people is their impatience with negative thinking and negative acting people. As you grow, your associates will change. Some of your friends will not want you to go on. They will want you to stay where they are. Friends that don›t help you climb will want you to crawl. Your friends will stretch your vision or choke your dream. Those that don›t increase you will eventually decrease you.

Consider this:

Never receive counsel from unproductive people. Never discuss your problems with someone incapable of contributing to the solution, because those who never succeed themselves are always first to tell you how. Not everyone has a right to speak into your life. You are certain to get the worst of the bargain when you exchange ideas with the wrong person. Don't follow anyone who's not going anywhere.

With some people you spend an evening: with others you invest it. Be careful where you stop to inquire for directions along the road of life. Wise is the person who fortifies his life with the right friendships. If you run with wolves, you will learn how to howl. But, if you associate with eagles, you will learn how to soar to great heights. A mirror reflects a man's face, but what he is really like is shown by the kind of friends he chooses.

The simple but true fact of life is that you become like those with whom you closely associate - for the good and the bad. Be not mistaken. This is applicable to family as well as friends. Yes...do love, appreciate and be thankful for your family, for they will always be your family no matter what. Just know that they are human first and though they are family to you, they may be a friend to someone else and will fit somewhere in the criteria above.

In prosperity our friends know us; in adversity
We know our friends.

Never make someone a priority when
You are only an option for them.

If you are going to achieve excellence in big things,
You develop the habit in little matters.

Excellence is not an exception;
It is a prevailing attitude...

— General Colin L. Powell, USA (Ret.)

General Colin Luther Powell is an American statesman and a retired four-star general in the United States Army. Gen. Powell was born in Harlem, a neighborhood in the New York City borough of Manhattan, to Jamaican immigrant parents. He was educated in New York City graduating from a public high school and earning a Bachelor of Science in Geology from City College and later a Master of Business Administration from George Washington University. After distinguished commands in the U.S. Army, Powell became the 65th United States Secretary of State (2001-2005), the first African American appointed to that position. During his military career, Powell also served as National Security Advisor (1987-1989), as Commander of the U. S. Army Forces Command (1989), and as Chairman of the Joint Chiefs of Staff (1989-1993), holding the latter position during the Gulf War. He was the first, and so far the only, African American to serve on the Joint Chiefs of Staff. In 1997 America's Promise Alliance was founded with Gen. Powel as Chairman. The alliance, presently chaired by Alma Powell, is a cross-sector partnership of 400+ corporations, nonprofits, faith-based organizations, and advocacy groups that are passionate about improving lives and changing outcomes for children. A primary function of the alliance is engaging in advocacy to provide children and young people with key support called "Five Promises: caring adults, safe places, a healthy start, an effective education and opportunities to help others."

PUBLISHER'S PREFACE

A Two-sided Problem

At-risk Youth

Dealing with at-risk youth is a two-sided problem. When one attempts to unlock the antecedent causes and the anticipated remedial action required to both prevent and rehabilitate at-risk youth, the problem becomes almost unsolvable. This two-sided difficulty must be separated into the past, present, and the future. Each aspect of the difficulty must be reviewed and evaluated based on a realistic intake assessment of the present situation of the client. Mentoring can only deal with the rehab aspects of the difficulty. Prevention is a whole other can of worms. The individuals and circumstances that created the problem in the first place must be addressed by others. Since the old adage, "An ounce of prevention is worth a pound of cure" is true, a big question is obvious: why were the prevention steps not taken?

A Gigantic Task

Unlocking the future for an at-risk youth is a gigantic task, but it must be tackled, confronted, endured, in the same way one would climb a difficult hill, weather a great storm, or eat an elephant (one bite at a time). Why is this difficult process necessary? It is perhaps the last best chance to give the young person, and society, the possibility for a better future. Youth mentoring starts with the present, but must deal with the past and the future.

Painstaking Patience and Endurance

Mentoring deals with an intake "snapshot" of the at-risk person and frames it in three dimensions of time and space: past, present, and future. The hard part begins when the Mentor attempts to make minor adjustments to the initial "snapshot" image. There are no computer programs with an automatic correction button. Painstaking patience and endurance on the part of both the Mentor and the Mentee must occur over time to move the process forward and understand the portrait in the context of the present state of the young person. There are only a few tools in the Mentor's snapshot correction box. These tools work best when the Mentor has sufficient background data to understand how past experiences inform the present state. Background data enables the creation of a future portrait as to how the Mentee would look at the end of the mentoring process. This would be a composite and an idyllic portrayal of a young person facing the future with hope and confidence. How would this process work?

A Mental Snapshot

After reviewing intake data about the past and a present interview with the client to create a mental snapshot of the Mentee, the Mentor would begin making corrections and alterations to the intake snapshot. Attempts at red face removal to eliminate the shame and embarrassment of being subjected to counseling and mentoring are the first steps. Then the Mentor would compare and contrast the real life situation of the at-risk client with an ideal or textbook case of mature young people who are well-adjusted emotionally and socially. At this point the Mentor may try enlarging the picture, then a little rotation to give a different perspective and finally some cropping of the snapshot to find the hidden elements that could be enlarged into a more mature lifestyle for the young person.

A Trial and Error Process

The process may be trial and error but the procedures cannot be freeze framed into a one-size-fits-all strategy. The mentoring process remains one-on-one and each case is different. The Mentor is always searching for a composite picture for the future that resembles the young person. The resemblance must be sufficient for the client to easily identify with the composite image. When the client begins to see the possibility of becoming the person described in the portrait by the Mentor, the work of mentoring is on track to provide the young person with a hopeful future.

An Over Simplification

Parenting and the home environment are normally blamed for the troubles experienced by young people. This is an over simplification. The record demonstrates that good parents can have troubled children. Also, it is obvious that good children often come from less than perfect parenting and schooling. The community, the school, the 24/7 media, the Internet, drugs and the criminal element share the blame with the environment. The issue is not whom society will blame, but how can the circumstances be altered that put young people at-risk? Perhaps a start in the right direction would be better parenting, better diets, better schools, better communities, more discipline, more adult interest in education, more jobs for young people, less exposure to the sexual revolution, less crime and violence, less exposure to drugs and the criminal element, and certainly less TV watching, less cell phone use, and less Internet surfing. Perhaps more faith-based teaching could be a factor in changing the environment.

Part of the Solution

This book is part of the solution. It is based on academic research and a structured analysis of at-risk young people in Trinidad and Tobago that culminated in a National Mentoring Program. In 2007 following a Public Consultations on Crime, it was recommended that a structured program be launched whereby trained personnel would provide one-on-one mentoring to youth-at-risk. A government leader's advisory, by Cabinet minutes, established an Inter-Ministerial Committee comprising five (5) stakeholder Ministries to develop a Structured Mentoring Program for Youth-at-Risk. The program is under the auspices of the Ministry of National Security; other Ministries involved are:

- People and Social Development

- Education

- Sports and Youth Affairs

- Science, Technology & Tertiary Education

In 2011, the author, as a consultant to the Ministry of National Security, presented a draft Operational Manual and other materials for government approval. The purpose of the material was to provide a common framework, based on best practice principles in support of a National Mentorship Program.

What Works Here would Work Elsewhere

Trinidad and Tobago appears to be a microcosm of the Caribbean region and a functioning example of a small nation. It is assumed that a National Mentorship Program that works here would probably work elsewhere. This developing nation has a diverse population and a mix of ethnicity, religion, cultural and social strata, together with communication technology that links to global and geo-political alliances. This has impacted the structure, attitude, and performance of primary units of socialization resulting in a breakdown of families, morality, and spiritual values. All this has produced underachieving young people and the antecedents to youth becoming at-risk.

Part of the Rationale

Both the opportunity and challenges became part of the rationale for this book. The underlying justification for the book came from an increase in single parenting, decrease in extended family networks, and technological innovations. It became clear that the family and the community, normally the providers of social capital, no longer were able to provide the necessary support for a growing youth population. The mentoring program was designed to act as a support system to at-risk young people who experience these challenges. Consequently, the focus of the mentoring program included dropout prevention, job training, school retention, basic literacy, community development, as well as the prevention of substance abuse, teen pregnancy and violence and crime. The basic objective is to develop a mentoring program where the Mentor becomes both a friend and role model to support and encourage the Mentee in holistic development.

Research and National Consultancy Available

The author of the research that established the basis for the National Mentorship Program in Trinidad and Tobago is available to assist other nations in the greater Caribbean region. She and her staff would be privileged to have the opportunity to assist other entities in the region in establishing a National Mentoring Initiative. Having served as a consultant to the Ministry of National Security in structuring the national mentoring policy, the author is available to governments, corporations, and private efforts to consult on the matter of initiating a mentoring effort. This consultancy is to provide a common framework, based on best practice principles to support and inform the design and development of a National Mentorship Policy. Literature and programmatic tools are available; such as, brochures, operational manuals, and promotional pieces to meet the needs of clients. Write to *ConsultOnYouth@gmail.com* for more information.

—Hollis L. Green, ThD, PhD

CHAPTER ONE

The Mission of Mentoring

National Youth Mentoring

The mission of a national youth mentoring initiative would be to reduce delinquency, gang participation, use of illegal drugs, and school failure or dropout, and increase self-awareness and self-confidence through one-on-one mentoring of at-risk youth. A national mentoring endeavor must accomplish several goals: (1) provide the resources and personnel to guide at-risk youth; (2) stimulate both personal and social responsibility among at-risk youth; (3) enhance the ability of at-risk youth to increase participation in education; (4) discourage delinquent activity such as violence and the use of illegal drugs by at-risk youth; and (5) guide at-risk youth in the participation in socially fulfilling activities. At lease, two or more of these goals must be reached to assure a worthwhile endeavor.

Guidance and Coaching

Mentoring is the guidance and coaching by an experienced advisor of a younger or less experienced individual. In the case of this book, the concept of youth ranges from adolescence to the older teen years. This age cohort experiences apprehension and nervousness about the future and becomes easily disturbed or distressed about problematic events characterized by difficulties or adversity. This makes this age grouping prone to emotional conflict or psychological difficulties. This is often precipitated by a dysfunctional family, a crime ridden region, poor performance in school, or peer pressure to become involved with illegal drugs or criminal activity. Other than the difficulty of dysfunctional parents, youthful delinquency becomes the major cause of criminal activity and unacceptable behavior in a given community. A powerlessness to function emotionally and socially in the community is the primary reason for the intervention of mentoring at-risk youth.

Informal Relationships

Most mentoring relationships are informal, and develop on the basis of mutual identification and the fulfillment of obvious needs. The Mentor may see the young person, whose present difficulties hide his or her excellent but undeveloped qualities, while the youth may view the Mentor as a competent role model with valued knowledge, skills, and abilities. Individuals guiding young people often report mutual areas of interest that spark the mentoring relationship. This enables them to provide both coaching and protection from adverse forces that create an environment that fosters possibilities and a hopeful future. The Mentor also provides personal support, friendship, counseling, acceptance, and role modeling. Each mentor-ing relationship is different and roles may vary on a case by case basis.

Phases of Mentoring

Mentoring and coaching relationships pass through several phases: (1) there is the initial contact to get acquainted, (2) then comes a nurturing process to build a relationship and to enable the young person to grow and develop personally. After a period of time there will be a (3) separation, either because the youth no longer needs the mentor or because of other interventions; such as, changing schools, family moving away, or the mentor comes to the conclusion that the relationship has accomplished its purpose. Regardless, eventually there will be a separation and a need to (4) redefine the relationship will becomes evident. Obviously, a mentoring process is time sensitive and cannot last forever, the young person must begin to stand on his or her own feet and the Mentor will move on to provide assistance to others. Either the Mentor becomes a caring friend at a distance or the relationship is terminated. This becomes a judgment call based on the family environment, maturity and problem-solving skills of the client.

Mentoring Troubled Youth means:

Mentoring and coaching the inexperienced

Engaging the youth at their point of need

Nurturing and navigating through difficulties

Tutoring and guiding in problem-solving skills

Opening doors for future opportunities

Reducing dysfunctional activity and attitudes

Increasing positive social involvement

Negotiating an agreement through discussion

Gaining self-confidence and self-awareness

Mentoring is Collaboration

The research supporting this book suggested the need for the implementation of a national mentoring program for youths in difficult circumstances. The program should be executed in collaboration with Government Organizations and the private sector. The program will facilitate at-risk youth in finding the right individuals to guide them through various difficulties and required transitions. The research suggested that this effort must be a highly structured program since the identification of proper role models were apparently challenging. One must consequently apply a rigid selection process in securing those who would mentor. Such a program can also provide dual mentoring relationships where youths can benefit from the learning experiences of both male and female role models. This concept is to provide the youth with an adult who can act as a friend, a confidant, coach and role model for a crucial period of time.

A Sustained Relationship

The concept of mentoring comes from the Greek word meaning "enduring" and is defined as a "sustained relationship between a youth and an adult." Through continued involvement, the adult offers support, guidance, and assistance as the younger person goes through a difficult period, faces new challenges, or works to correct earlier problems. In particular, where parents are either unavailable or unable to provide the required responsible guidance, the role of mentoring plays a critical role in improving the self-awareness, self-image, and personal behavior of at-risk youth. The two types of mentoring are **natural mentoring** and **planned mentoring**. Natural mentoring occurs through friendship, collegiality, teaching, coaching, and counseling. In contrast, planned mentoring occurs through structured programs in which adults and youth are selected and matched through a formal process.

Popularity of Mentoring Programs

Mentoring programs grew dramatically in the past decade. Most of the popularity comes from positive tributes from both young people and adult mentors who witnessed the benefits of mentoring. Mentors saw the positive influences of coaching and mentoring programs that assisted young people with their self-concept, personal confidence, problem-solving skills, and generally improved their personal and social proficiency.

Why Initiate Mentoring Programs?

Research data from various sources have produced compelling evidence that positive role models have a significant result in a one-on-one relationship between youth and an adult. The need is created by the number of dysfunctional families, communities filled with crime and drugs, negative peer influence, and general at-risk behavior of unsupervised and immature youth. The need for mature adult mentoring is compounded by absentee parents, school drop-outs, unwed teenage pregnancy, and the increase use of illegal drugs.

Mentoring Interventions

Coaching and mentoring interventions are instituted to provide at-risk youth a process to reduce the impact of delinquency and increase the problem-solving skills. The presence of a mature and experienced adult to build a positive relationship with at-risk young people has a validated benefit of reducing the negative and increasing the positive in relationship to the specific needs of an individual client.

A Primary Goal

Matching a suitable mentor with an at-risk youth is a primary goal of mentoring programs. Different programs have various selection procedures for mentors and clients. Normally, a media search finds appropriate individuals with both a "heart" for young people and the "time" to volunteer to assist with mentoring. A goal is to create a natural surrogate relationship to replace the limited parenting and negative influence of the local environment on at-risk youth. This must be a mutually agreed on process to produce positive results.

At-risk Youth

This is not a derogatory term, but a realistic assessment of the dangers of being young and inexperienced. Almost all children and young people are subject to negative influence in the present society. Both in the home and the community, they are exposed to unconstructive influences. With both parents working added to the single parent families, the young are susceptible to pessimistic and downbeat attitudes. In addition to the normal pressures of growing up, crime, drugs and other delinquents impose peer pressure on the young. The idea of mentoring troubled youth in no way is meant to be offensive, but is designed to face the reality of the needs of the present generation. This age cohort normally listens more to peers than to parents, teachers, or religious leaders. This is a good reason for mentoring programs that build self-esteem and problem solving skills.

Scholars Disagree

Although scholars do not always agree on the process of development or corrective measures when youth go astray, they normally agree that there are critical periods in the development of children and young people. Most agree that the young need guidance and when parents and/or educational institutions fail to provide this assistance, programs such as mentoring become useful. Culture becomes an important environmental factor in developing the young. Europe and the United States maintain individualistic cultures and emphasize individual needs. In contrast, Asia, Africa, Central and South America are characterized by community-centric cultures that focus on belonging to a larger group, such as family or nation. Ethnicity is also a factor and provides mores, customs, and traditions. In such cultures, cooperation with a group is often more important than individual growth. This is another area where mentoring can be useful in keeping young people on the right track.

Mentoring May be a Solution

Among the most destructive things that can happen to young people is to become socially involved with peers who have bad habits, immoral behavior and weak character. In the general population it is difficult to restrict these associations, because restriction has the reverse effect. This means that the associations of children and adolescents must be monitored and each negative incident promptly dealt with by a loving parent. Constructive communication is crucial at this point. When parents or guardians are unable to correct bad behavior, the mentoring concept may be a solution. A grounded program of mentoring and coaching can be a most helpful process for parents and families.

Delinquents from the Street

Sadly, young people listen to delinquents from the street instead of following the guidance of parents or guardians. Since it is obvious that some young people will need positive guidance and assistance outside the home and school environment, the initiating of a national or community program of mentoring can become a positive influence on family and national stability. With both parents working and children and young people being without adequate supervision for part of the day or night, the beneficial aspects of mentoring programs become obvious. As General Powell said, "The simple but true fact of life is that you become like those with whom you closely associate - for the good and the bad." Mentoring can assist parents and guardians in pointing young people in the right direction.

Dimensions of Mentoring

There are both practical and spiritual dimensions to the mentoring process. The adults who function as mentors deal with both the academic and personal aspects of young people. Those who learn to listen, analyze and act positively are able to benefit troubled youth and guide them to a pathway that leads to progress and personal achievements. Dealing with difficult situations requires, not only a knowledge of human development, but also the nature of spiritual development. The goal is to instill in each young person a confident and positive attitude about the future. Perhaps a brief prayer once painted on a small stone could shed light on such a positive attitude:

Lord, help me to remember that
Nothing will happen to me today
That you and I together can't handle!

CHAPTER TWO

National At-risk Youth

Delinquent and Criminal Systems

Delinquency and crime among young people have been on the rise in most communities. There is a growing need to identify effective programs to teach problem solving skills for youth in difficult situations. Family instability, lack of employment opportunities and the inability of the education system to provide for the needs of youth in challenging situations seem to be overwhelming. The problems span from poor economic conditions to an abusive home environment. For troubled youth, the path to a positive support system may appear too difficult to negotiate; thus, they resort to easily accessible schemes that appear ready to meet their needs. It is this negative process that mentoring programs attempt to prevent from happening. The delinquent and criminal systems in the community are a major disadvantage to at-risk youth.

What can be Done?

The transitional period from childhood to adulthood is unquestionably another challenge faced by many young people. However, their successful navigation of this period hinges on the support and guidance received from individuals, families and society at large. Undeniably, policy-makers must play a pivotal role in improving the impact of this transition period on those faced with social and economic challenges. The increase in youth crime, drug use and high incidence of HIV signals that intervention is needed. We therefore must ask ourselves: 'what can we do?'

Psycho-social and Socio-economic Factors

Within recent years, attention has been increasingly focused on problems of youth crime, academic performance, substance abuse and other issues related to young persons. Research suggests that these youth and their families have multiple needs and interrelated problems that are not likely to be successfully addressed by any single response. There is therefore growing interest in collaborative approaches to address these multiple needs. Further to this, youth in difficult circumstances are usually branded by many sections of society as trouble makers and delinquents. They have therefore become the lens through which all young people are viewed. This study took an opposing stance in seeking to highlight youth as potentially productive social actors who adopt certain skills to survive in an unfriendly environment. The study examined the psycho-social and socio-economic factors that lead to youth delinquency.

Focus on East Trinidad

The purpose of this study was to identify the adequacy of problem solving skills utilized by youth in difficult circumstances with a focus on youth in East Trinidad. It was envisaged that this book would stimulate on-going discussions and provide information, which would serve as the basis for the development and operationalization of initiatives intended to address effective problem solving skill for youth in difficulty.

Effective Strategies

The research not only identified the factors that gave rise to difficult circumstances among youth and the adequacy of their problem solving skill, but also determined effective problem-solving skills that assisted youth in these situations. It provided a situational analysis of youth in difficult circumstances in the population studied, but the findings may be generalized to the Caribbean region and other small countries. It examined the policies and programs of government and non-government organizations that have been introduced to address youth in difficult situations and suggested additional effective strategies to solve problems of troubled youth.

This study was designed to satisfy the following objectives.

- To identify key factors facing youth in difficult circumstances.

- To identify the adequacy of the problem solving skills utilized by youth.

- To examine the support available through policies and programs to youth in difficult circumstances.

- To recommend effective strategies to assist youth in effective problem solving.

Definition of Concepts

The following concepts were given operational definitions and were interpreted as described below:

Youth – poised uneasily between the world of childhood and that of an adult, the youth are seen as going through a period of extreme psychological and social upheaval, rocked by the onslaught of hormonal changes on the one hand, and by rebellion against values and judgments of the grown-up world on the other. (Varma 1997).

One of the challenges in working with youth is defining who they are. (United Nations Children's Fund 2002) defines youth as those individuals between the ages, 15-24 years.

There are also variations between the concept of adolescence, youth, and what constitutes young people. The definition is further confused by the fact that in many parts of the world, youth may not be determined by age. Youth is considered "a time of passage between childhood and adulthood" (Office of Conflict Management and Mitigation 2005). In some cultures, male and female initiation rites mark the passage from childhood to adulthood. In others, females are only considered "youth' before marriage, an event that in some cultures can occur at an early age; therefore, being categorized early in life as young adults and no longer youth. (Newman, 2005) The concept of youth is intrinsically linked to the transition from childhood to adulthood, from a stage where the individual needs protection and guidance to one of independence and self-determination. Thus, the term "youth" can therefore be paradoxical. Defining who they are can therefore be an argument in itself. This study adopted as a cohort, ages 12-19.

Difficult Circumstances --The term was coined by the UNICEF (1980's) during the time of an increase in street children. The term was originally established to include refugees, children with disabilities, working children and street children. However, the term is now widely used throughout the world. The term 'difficult circumstances' could now be used to refer to a number of specific social circumstances which includes children who do not live with their families, who work in abusive conditions, or are involved in armed conflict. The term in most literature seems to be almost synonymous with street children. These children have suffered prolonged deprivation, family violence and live in poor economic situations and therefore turn to the streets to survive.

As society becomes globalize, there is a wider gap between the rich and the poor. The less fortunate youth therefore become excluded, exposing them to a number of additional difficult circumstances. This evolution gave rise for the broadening of the term. The term now includes children who are victim of AIDS and those who at an early age are expected to earn a living to care for themselves and their families. This study will refer to youth in difficult circumstances as youth who are exposed to the various types of social circumstances, which includes those specific circumstances identified above.

Problem-solving Skills -- is generally referred to as a tool, a skill and a process. It is a tool as it can help solve a problem; a skill because once learned it can be repeatedly used, and a process as it involves taking a number of steps. Youth in difficult circumstances face a series of challenges which often call for decision making. Some decisions are as simple as deciding what to eat or what to wear. However, most decisions require much more skill. When confronted with challenging circumstances it becomes difficult for youth to decide on the best options.

Unless these youth are provided with the support needed during their difficult circumstances they will be unable to effectively solve any problem. This support will necessitate resources such as access to employment and equal opportunities. Consequently, these would help them alleviate their problems of poverty, unemployment and other socioeconomic conditions that exclude them from effectively functioning in society.

Population -- In Trinidad and Tobago, there are approximately 400,000 children, adolescents, youth, and young adults.   According to the information received from the Crime and Problem Analysis Branch (2005-2006), youths between the ages of twelve and eighteen years committed one hundred and thirty one,(131) robberies, ninety nine, (99) larceny and four hundred and forty two, (442) narcotic offences. It is this cohort that concerns this work. The same office further indicates that youth between the ages nineteen and twenty nine years, during the same period, committed two hundred and sixty one (261) robberies, two thousand and eighty two (2082) narcotic offences and five hundred and fourteen, (514) larceny. However, these figures represent only those youth who are arrested and charged. The actual numbers of youth who engage in these crimes are therefore not truly reflected in this data. Consequently, to prevent the younger cohort (12-18) from moving into the higher category is the reason for targeting them with a national mentoring initiative.

According to the Trinidad and Tobago Central Statistical Office youth in Trinidad and Tobago experience poverty to a greater extent than other population groups. The changes in the family composition and migration have contributed to the reduced support for youth within the family. In some cases families have relinquished their parental responsibilities altogether, leaving children in the care of government supported institutions which have their own developmental risk factors. Youth in poor communities face additional challenges, such as, exclusion, abuse and neglect; this is further compounded by limited employment opportunities. Reduced family support place the youth in difficult circumstances, more so, those from poor communities and thus contributes to higher manifestations of behavioral problems, such as crime and delinquency.

The proportion of violent crimes committed by young people has been increasing. The problem has also been reflected in the growing increase in school violence. During a recent Senate budget consideration, it was noted that Afro-Trinidadian youth in the east/west corridor had a propensity to become involved in criminal activity. However, research has shown that the problem does not lie only among Afro-Trinidadians nor is it restricted to the east/west corridor. The formation of school gangs has been nationwide. Recent media reports have highlighted an increasing number of gang violence in schools in North and South Trinidad as well as the East. The reports have identified children of both East Indian and African descent as perpetrators of school violence. There is concern with what has caused this increase and why young people fall prey.

According to the (United Nations Report), two factors contribute to social problems in Trinidad and Tobago. They are flawed education system and unemployment. The flawed education system refers to the structure of the education system and its inability to address specific needs of youth in difficult circumstances. While these may indeed be contributory factors, they are not the only hindrances experienced by youth. The migration of parents, abuse and poor economic situations further exasperate their situation.

Several youths are therefore dropouts from school with little or no education and are attempting to find employment. They spent most of their time on the street with their peers and often found themselves engaging in unlawful activities. Additionally, some youths found themselves in difficult circumstances in their immediate environment as they were subject to migrating families and abuse in different forms. The situational analysis revealed that these conditions led youths to resort to a number of illegal activities to survive. These included bullying and petty crimes. This concern led the government and Non- governmental organizations to the development of a number of youth policies and youth programs that caters particularly to out of school youth.

CHAPTER THREE

Policies and Youth Powerlessness

Youth Powerlessness

The (Trinidad and Tobago Youth and Social Development Report 2000), stated that during a period of economic prosperity, youth unemployment remained at 30 percent. The Government of Trinidad and Tobago and private organizations made several attempts to respond to the problems of youth unemployment. Strategies used include the formulation of youth policies and the introduction of a number of programs to assist in youth development. These consist of several training program as outlined below.

Civilian Conservation Corps (CCC)

The CCC program falls under the Ministry of National Security and commenced on 14th June, 1993 embracing both male and female young people. This program provides attitudinal and skills development training to young adults between the ages of eighteen and twenty five years. The programs focuses on entrepreneurship, self discipline and care for the environment. Selection to the program is based on a grading system which is determined by the extent of vulnerability to which an individual is exposed. This means that all youth in difficult circumstances may not necessarily qualify for the program but rather those who are considered to be in extreme difficult circumstances. These trainees are given a stipend of seventy dollars a day.

This six month program is conducted in three phases. The induction phase addresses gender issues, career guidance and life skills. The transformation phase concentrates on environmental and agro projects and skills training such as masonry, welding and food preparation. Phase three of the program is the refreezing phase which addresses assimilation of the previous phases.

In March, 1999 the program was suspended, but was reopened in April, 2002. The program has since changed structure to accommodate the changing needs of these youths. It has included marketable skills such as computer literacy, culinary arts and beauty culture. Trainees are exposed to the world of work by participating in On the Job Training (OJT), and were also expanded to areas in central and south, having previously been available only in north Trinidad.

There is, however, a perception among young people that participation in this program as a prerequisite to enter the Defense Force. Only a small percentage of the youth who participate in the program actually gain entry to the Defense Force according to data from the Civilian Conservation Corps. This reality can be disappointing to the youth and usually discourages them from participating. Further to this, at the end of the program the youth return to their environment faced with the same situation of unemployment. There is no follow-up at the end of the program to determine the level of success or the challenges of participants. There are also no provisions made for further employment or support.

Helping Youth Prepare for Employment (HYPE)

HYPE program began in 2002 catering to nationals between seventeen to twenty five years of age. The program accommodates youth with at least post- primary education and who are unable to find employment, equipping them with skills in the construction industry. Upon completion of the training, participants receive certification from the National Training Agency. These youths become marketable in the construction field and their certification is recognized by most construction firms. Participants received a stipend of fifty dollars from August 2007. There are presently six centers, one in Tobago and five throughout Trinidad. Unfortunately, the centers are not evenly distributed throughout the island so persons in remote areas are at a disadvantage.

The HYPE program requires youth to have some level of literacy attainment, yet this is not stipulated as a criterion for entry. Thus, youths who are unable to cope with the level of work offered usually drop out. Participants of the program who live in remote areas also find it difficult to meet the costs of transportation. This has also resulted in a high dropout rate. Youth in difficult circumstances may be exposed to all of these constraints, thereby limiting them from benefiting fully from the program. The program has therefore gained little success in addressing youth in difficulty.

The Geriatric Adolescents Partnership Program (GAPP)

This program was designed to sensitize young individuals between the ages seventeen to twenty five years to the aging process and help to bridge the gap between the young and old while developing practical skills in geriatric care. The program has both a practical and theoretical component and provides the youth with skills for self employment. Individuals are given a stipend of sixty dollars a day during training. This program began in December, 1993 as a six month pilot project under the Ministry of Community Development, Culture and Gender Affairs. Youths who participate in this program are expected to find employment in elderly Homes or open their own Home. The truth is, many of these youths cannot be absorbed in care centers due to inadequate spaces and in many cases, lack of funding, prevent them from opening their own business. They therefore complete the course and while some find jobs within agencies a number of them are unable to gain employment.

Multi-Sector Skill Training (MUST)

MUST is a specialized craft training program that seeks to develop individuals in areas of construction and hospitality. It is a six month program and caters to persons between eighteen to fifty years of age. The program started in July, 2004 with level-one training. From the year 2006, level-two was introduced; these persons are now able to become more specialized in a skill. Participants are trained in tile-laying, masonry, hospitality and are also exposed to life skills training. In August 2007, the daily stipend of sixty dollars was increased to eighty dollars to cushion the impact of the   increases in cost of living and transportation. It is anticipated that persons who enter the program are desirous of learning a skill. Some youths find entry into the MUST program a challenge, because they must satisfy a series of entry requirements. One such requirement is that the individual must be drug free. This prerequisite deterred a large number of youths. In order to encourage participation in the program, a new program was introduced to encourage youths to abstain from drug use. This program was called Positively Altering Life Style (PALS). This new program was piloted in March 2007 and was four month duration. Unfortunately, even though mechanisms are being put in place to sustain the MUST program, exclusion due to drug use persists.

On the other hand, successful applicants to the MUST program, complain of sexual exploitation of young ladies. The young men also complain of exploitation on the job, as they are asked to perform task that is not related to their area of training. For example, they may be asked to clean drains. These situations discourage the youths from completing the training program and a number of them eventually drop out.

The Non-Traditional Skills Training Program

This program was designed to provide specialized technical and vocational education to low income women between the ages of eighteen and fifty years. The program was initiated in 1998 under the Ministry of Community Development, Culture and Youth Affairs. Young women bene-fited from the program by accessing courses in domestic appliance repairs, small engine repairs, construction skills and upholstery. These areas were previously dominated by men. Participants were given a daily stipend of twenty dollars, however this recently increased to fifty then sixty dollars in response to economic demands. Recently, gloves, booths and helmets were issued in accordance with the OSHA Act. In order to increase accessibility to the program babysitting services are now offered to participants with young children and half of the cost for these services is met by the government. Additionally, transportation is provided for persons living in remote areas.

Although the program addresses gender issues, there are still challenges for the woman attempting to survive in a man's market. As such, participants in the program are encouraged to form groups and open their own business. They are given a grant of up to sixty percent of the project cost from the Community Development Fund to furbish this business. However, unresolved disputes among individuals breakdown in communication and inability to function as a team often results in the eventual abortion of the business plan. The program therefore needs to address conflict management and team-building as skill-building compo-nents for these young people. If an individual decides to be a sole trader, she experiences two problems, fear of failing in a male dominated market and lack of funding to establish the business as a sole trader.

The On-The Job Training (OJT)

OJT was initiated in 1980   under the National Training Board, providing training for persons desiring entry into the job market. The program, then called National Apprenticeship System existed for sixteen years and closed in 1996.

The pre-employment training program offers participation and induction into the world of work and focuses on educational and occupational skills. It gives youth between the ages sixteen to thirty years, experience in the working world. The program was restructured in the year 2002 under the Ministry of Science and Technology. Individuals were placed for a period of six months in an organization for a forty- hour work week and were paid no less than the minimum hourly wage. The wage differs according to the level of education the trainee had attained. A trainee with Advanced level education therefore received more than someone with Ordinary level education. The program was again restructured in May 2007, facilitating individuals up to the age of thirty five years. Older persons who had not been exposed to the job market were given an opportunity to develop new skills. The period of job placement for on the job trainees was increased from six months to twelve months. The longer training period enhanced the trainee's ability to further developing their skills base.

The program has its advantages in that it provides a wide spectrum of learning skills to persons in different fields of work. Some trainees who worked well are given the opportunity to maintain their position in the work place as some employers screen employees for permanent jobs through this system.

On the other hand, because of the extensive demand for the program, job spaces are limited. As a result, a number of individuals are denied access to the program. Youth in difficult circumstances are severely unable to satisfy the entry level requirements due to their low level of education.

Youth Training and Employment Partnership Program (YTEPP)

YTEPP was implemented in August, 1987 as a pilot project. The program was commissioned by the then Ministry of Planning and Reconstruction and was managed by the Department of Extra Mural Studies, the University of the West Indies. The program was officially launched as a short term intervention to assist in the serious social challenge of youth unemployment. It comprised of six projects at forty centers throughout the nation. In 1998, the first community based training program was launched in Moruga, offering training for nine months and facilitating youth in rural areas. The program continued to develop new strategies to address changing needs of youth and advancement in technology.

YTEPP provides training to young people between the ages of fifteen to twenty five years who had dropped out of school and these individuals are trained in areas of Career enhancement, Literacy Skills, Vocational Skills Training and Entrepreneurial development. Participants of the program receive a daily stipend of twenty four dollars which has since August, 2007 increased to sixty dollars.

Some obstacles that prevent youth from benefiting from this program are the late hours of classes which are held in secondary schools and which have to be conducted between the hours of 3.00 pm to 7.00 pm and 5.30 pm to 9.00 pm. The late hours have not attracted many as it has proven to be a challenge to youth in rural areas. There is also a stigma attached to YTEPP as the program first catered to individuals who have dropped out of primary schools. This stigma, to date, has left a negative impact and because of this, youth disassociate themselves from the program. In spite of this, the program officer indicated that yearly, the program surpassed the organization's target with a sixty five percent success rate. This means that there are many youths who access the program and benefit from it

The Military-Led Academic Training (MILAT) and Military-Led Youth Program of Apprenticeship and Reorientation Training (MYPART)

MILAT and MYPART are the two most recent youth programs launched 2nd May, 2007 with eighty eight trainees. These programs are two and three year live-in programs, they are respectively designed to empower "at risk' youths. They aim to instill positive attitudinal and behavioral change while providing the opportunity for academic, technical and vocational qualifications. The criterion for entry is youth who have been termed 'at risk'. Participants are to receive a stipend of forty dollars a day; however, they have not yet received it. This stipend is small, but these youths are provided with all basic necessities during their institutionalization. It should be noted that participation in the program is not a criterion for entry in the military.

The MILAT program is academic based and trains students to write four subjects at the Caribbean Secondary Examination Council (CSEC) exams. These subjects include Math and English. The MYPART program caters for those whose interest is in technical work but trainees are also expected to do Math and English. These two programs are only months old, so it may be difficult to assess their impact at this stage. However, the program presently facilitates only male youth. The program director has included a number of projects within the program to assist the youth as they make the transition to the working world. One such project is a Mentoring component. This component provides a mentor for each youth in the program. The mentor becomes a role model and guides this youth throughout the program. The mentor remains a friend and will assist the youth as he makes the transition to the working world or career enhancement.

Non- Government Organizations (NGO's) Response

A number of Non Governmental Organizations have also contributed to the development and empowerment of young people in difficult circumstances by providing training programs and care centers. I will make mention of three of these programs, namely Choices, Servol and YMCA.

Choices

The program was initiated by the Child Welfare League of Trinidad and Tobago, Ministry of Health, and Bernard Van Leer Foundation. It was established in January, 1994 to address the concerns of teenage parenting. The program, since 2005, began to receive a quarterly grant from the government. The criteria for entry are single teenage mothers, pregnant teenagers and teenagers at risk. These teenagers are taught academics, family life education and skills training from 9 am to 3 pm, Monday to Friday. These teenagers are provided with a nursery facility at the centre so they can care for their children while learning other skills. The participants are given support through counselors who will assess their needs and make referrals to other agencies. This assistance is not always provided in the form of money but through other services rendered to them. The program initially had three centers. However, in October 2005, after the government assessed the program they requested that centers be opened throughout Trinidad and Tobago. As a result of this, one additional centre was opened in October 2005, in Laventille. Though this program structure is the same as the other programs there is a different financial arrangement. This arrangement allows participants from the Laventille program to receive a stipend of twenty dollars an hour. This is made possible through a yearly subvention from the Government, while the previously existing centers only receive a grant. This grant is a sum of money paid only when a particular request is made. It is not a continued sum of money that could facilitate a daily stipend. The management of the centers is however, making recommendations for an integration of the present program with the existing program which would allow participants of all centers to receive a stipend.

An assessment of the program revealed that most of these teenagers receive little or no support from their parents. In many cases they are abandoned by their parents when they become pregnant. Thus, they need additional support in finding a home and employment. To combat this problem, a number of them enter common law relationships where they submit to abuse, while few end up homeless. There is therefore need for a transitional residential facility to absorb youth who have little or no support.

Another area that should be addressed in this program is the enforcement of a policy by the Ministry of Education which allows teenagers to re-enter school after delivery of their babies. The social worker attached to the centre usually has to negotiate with the school's principal for this concession. This Ministry directive should not be ignored nor left to the discretion of the school's principal.

Servol

Servol is a non-governmental organization established in 1970 in the aftermath of the black power riots. The programs were developed based on ideas from the community. They initially started with two age groups, birth to five years old since these were the most critical years and the sixteen to nineteen years old that had either dropped out of or failed in formal education. The efforts of Servol in the sphere of early childhood care and education were enhanced through the support of the Bernard Van Leer foundation.

The adolescent program began as a traditional skill-training centre, on the assumption that once a young person was trained in a marketable skill, employment could be easily found. However, the initial results were disappointing, and a number of apprentices dropped out the program and some who completed returned to the streets attempting to fulfill their financial obligations and alleviate some of the hardship they experience. This gave rise to the need to develop a pre- vocational course thus the Adolescent Development Program was structured as a three and a half month course. In 1986, the Government asked Servol to disseminate its programs throughout the country. The expansion went ahead and to date, Servol oversees more than one hundred and eighty early childhood centers and thirty adolescent centers. The program has been able to reach youths in difficult circumstances throughout the country. However, youth in difficult circumstances to whom the program is designed for can barely afford to stay in the program. The program does not provide any transport assistance and the class of persons who attend this program usually have financial difficulties.

Young Men's Christian Association (YMCA)

The YMCA, a non- governmental organization, began its work in 1995 to assist youths in difficult circumstances. Their target population was young persons in high risk surroundings which may or may not include family support. The YMCA provides a drop- in -centre, offering counseling services, and training. It facilitates street children by providing bath, food, clothes, a non- threatening, youth friendly forum for ventilation and assistance in obtaining official documents, such as birth certificates. While its programs are well recognized for their intervention in youth-related problems, they are impeded by lack of human and financial support. The YMCA receives a Government subvention, but because of the immensity of the problems of youth, the organization has failed to effectively meet the needs of youth. Nevertheless, the program continues to assist where it can even though faced with difficulty to obtain professional staff with the little funding available. The organization is also challenged to identify sufficient care centers for youth in difficult circumstances.

Assessment of Youth Programs

In examining the initiatives taken it was realized that both Government and Non-Government organizations are addressing concerns of youth in difficult circumstances, and as a result there has been a proliferation of youth programs. These programs are aimed at teaching entrepreneurship and business skills to young people who may have been unsuccessful in their academic pursuits. However, there are a number of short falls that prevent youth from benefiting from these programs. The opportunities for young people, though expanded, have not sufficiently attracted youth in difficult circumstances. Communities where youths are vulnerable seem to lack the knowledge of what is available to them, how they can access it and how they can utilize it.

In many cases, the young people access programs that offer the highest stipend. Their concerns are more about alleviating their poor social conditions rather than gaining a skill. They therefore attempt to manipulate the system, accessing one program after the other benefiting only from the meager stipend that is given.

There also seems to be lack of consultation with youth to determine the types of programs that may interest them. There is also no guarantee of gaining employment after the training program, especially as generating income is of paramount important for the youth in difficult circumstances. It can also be noted that some trainees complain of being exploited during their job placement and therefore lose confidence in the system. In addition to this, skilled youths living in specific areas, such as Laventille are often discriminated against by employers because of their place of residence. They usually have to give false addresses if they want to succeed in gaining employment.

The criteria for entry into some programs also deprive youth from accessing the program, for example the drug testing in the MUST program prevents youth who may be using drugs. The literacy level expected in some programs also limits youth participation. There also seems to be a lack of monitoring and evaluation of these programs. Further, the implementation of appropriate policies to address the inadequacies in the system is severely lacking. It was also realized that there is an intervention gap between those children leaving primary school and those children who are suppose to be in secondary school. There are many children who leave primary school and never attend a secondary school either because of lack of financial resources or lack of academic ability. These children usually 'slip through the cracks', ignored by those who should be helping them. They more often than not, find themselves on the streets, liming with older friends and eventually become involved in unlawful activities. In addition to these shortfalls, there is insufficient research into the problems facing youth in difficult circumstances, and as a consequence there are inappropriate policies to address their difficulties.

CHAPTER FOUR

Education and Youth Difficulties

The Education System

The Trinidad and Tobago education system is centralized and so the Ministry of Education has the responsibility of all government schools. Some schools, though, are controlled by the denominational Board they do not strictly comply with Government Policy. The education of each child in Trinidad and Tobago is therefore greatly impacted by the policies implemented by the Government of Trinidad and Tobago.

The Common Entrance Examination is a method of determining entry to a stratified secondary structure. School places were short and this examination was used as a selection criterion for placing children in schools. According to the child's performance children were either placed in a seven year school, a five year school or a vocational school. The type of school the child attended was influenced by their learning abilities and greatly impacted on their outcome. The school system paid insufficient attention to school children in difficult circumstances and other educational problems of youth. It therefore became necessary for the education Ministry to establish a committee to address these problems.

Post primary centers were also set up to provide continuing education to those students who were not assigned to secondary school. According to the task force report, the program, although it sounds good in theory, in practice it did not live up to its expectations. The program failed to provide the type of interventions needed for special students. Children were therefore left in the post primary class with little intervention to empower them.

The (National Task Force on Education 1993-2003) was established to address the challenges faced by these 'at risk' youth. They reported that for the last two decades, the learning system has not sufficiently catered for those who are 'educationally at risk' or with special needs. The task force proposed the need to ensure smooth transition from primary to secondary level through diagnostic, remedial and developmental practices.

Out of this proposal, came the recommendation for transformation of common entrance into a national attainment test. Placement in secondary schools was recommended to be based on both continuous assessment and a national test. This policy was expected to remove the stress related to common entrance examination, therefore providing easier access for persons to obtain secondary level education.

In the year 2000, the Government introduced the Universal Secondary Education (USE)   placing all children who wrote the (SEA) secondary examination assessment exams in secondary schools. Additional support such as school transportation service of over two hundred maxi taxis and school buses, a school nutrition program providing breakfast and lunch to those from early childhood to secondary school, a text book rental program providing essential text books on loan and a book grant of one thousand dollars a student was provided for students.

The introduction of this policy caused a demand for increase spaces in secondary schools. Children who were not prepared for secondary schools were placed in secondary schools and were unable to academically perform. This situation caused some children to be lost in the system   since they could not cope with the work given. The children who were unable to cope with the school work found themselves engaging in other activities that were not part of the official school curriculum. This was a cause for concern as these activities usually encouraged delinquent and criminal behaviors

In 2007, the Government again reviewed the Education Policy for selecting primary school children for entry to secondary   school. This new policy allowed children who scored less than thirty percent in the examination and were over thirteen (13) years to enter secondary school, while giving an additional year to those who did not score over thirty percent and were under thirteen (13) years of age. It was intended that an additional year at the primary level would increase opportunities for success at the secondary level.

Review of Youth Difficulties

Much has been written on the challenges youths face. However, not enough has been done to address the psychosocial and socioeconomic factors that lead to delinquency among youth and to develop appropriate policies needed to assist them in problem solving. This review will examine the psychosocial and socioeconomic factors that lead to delinquent behaviors.

Discourses on youth include issues of teenage pregnancy, the spread of HIV, youth unemployment, youth and drugs, youth and crime, and the social exclusion of youth. Though many young people have been able to manage their difficult circumstances, there is an increasing recognition of those who may be unable to overcome the challenges.

These youths are referred to as 'youth- in- crisis', 'youth- at-risk', 'delinquent youth' or 'youth in difficult circumstances'. There are many predisposing factors which may be termed underlying issues to youth behavior.

The fact that many youth grow up in extremely difficult circumstances, leave us to wonder why some turn to violent and delinquent behavior and others do not. Researchers attribute a number of reasons for violent behaviors among youth. Some conclude that the majority of behaviors are explained by social factors, in other words, youths are not born violent but learn to be violent by seeing others use violence, and by themselves being victims of violence in their home and in their communities.

(Barker 2005) posits that though violence is not caused by poverty, it seems to be highest where there is inequality of income and social exclusion. Other researchers such as (Rodgers 1999) indicate that the breakdown of the family and lack of community cohesion contributes to violent behaviors. The World Health Organization in reviewing data concluded that youth violence is higher among young men when opportunities for employment are blocked.

(Danns et al 1977) referring to an article, 'The Social Reproduction of Youth in the Caribbean' contends that there is an increase in unacceptable behavior among the region's youth and concludes that no single agency of socialization can be held responsible for what the youths have become. This does not mean that there is no solution but implies that collaboration and networking of institutions is important in addressing the problems of youth. He further identifies peer groups as playing an increasingly influential role in shaping the emergence of new values among youth. Youth are a great influence to their peers as they spend a lot of time with them. Their thoughts, values and behaviors are shaped by their peers.

Stress among youth has also been noted as a contributor to violent behavior. (Barker 2005) alluded to the fact that youths who were subject to family stress such as breakdown in parental relationships, separation or living in abusive situations are likely to behave violently. In addition, (Crawford-Brown 1999) postulates that when families migrate, children struggle with feelings of rejection, abandonment and loss. Children are sometimes abandoned as early as months old and are separated from their parents for years. The child loses memory of the parents, then fear, anger and resentment step in, and the child then begins to act out anti-social tendencies.

Labeling

Labeling is also considered to be a major contributor to violent behavior among youth. (Haralambos and Holborn 2004) noted that there is no such thing as a deviant act; an act becomes deviant when others perceives it and labels it as a deviant act. Depending on who commits the act, when and where the act is committed the label will apply. Therefore, he concludes that the act of deviance does not lie in the behavior itself, but rather in the interaction between the persons who commit the act and those who respond to it. Further, she emphasized that these labels assigned to individuals largely override their other status. Since these individuals' self concepts are formed from the responses of others, they tend to see themselves in terms of the label.

Within the school system and at home, youth are constantly labeled. When young men are told by their parents, teachers and the media that they are violent, they become violent. Some young people are stigmatized due to their family background, peers with which they associate or things they have done in the past. This contributes to the labeling of youth. In spite of the youth's attempt to live differently, they are constantly faced with stigmatization from members of society. They eventually resort to the expected behavior as what we would refer to as self-fulfilling prophesy.

(Deosaran 2006), in his report on African youths in the East-West corridor indicates that for the past ten years several sectors of the national community have associated Afro-male youths along this area with committing violent crimes, facing the courts and ending up in prison. In fact, it seemed accepted as "fact" that these youth are a deviant lot, filled with criminal tendencies, active in crime and destined for prison. (Deosaran 2006).

He further indicates that people react to and treat with these youth on the basis of stereotyping. The treatment meted out to them is based on the perceptions they have of them, however wrong or right they may be. This means that people relate to one another largely on what they first imagine of them. Because of this, people fail to recognize the circumstances under which these youths live. They ignore their difficult circumstances and fail to acknowledge that these youth may be victims of poor economic situations.

Poor Economic Situations

Unemployment is regarded as one of the most challenging economic problem facing Government, in most Caribbean countries including Trinidad and Tobago. The unemployed in Trinidad and Tobago is defined to include "all persons who looked for work during a three month period preceding the enumeration and who at the time of enumeration did not have a job but still wanted work'(Trinidad and Tobago Central Statistical Office, 1995). This data has also shown that unemployment is higher among the female than the male. Data from CSO for July to September 2007 indicate that there is a 17.2 percentage of labor force of unemployed persons between the ages fifteen years to nineteen years, 8.1 percent for persons twenty to twenty four years and 7.1 percent between the ages twenty five to twenty nine years (Trinidad and Tobago Central Statistical Office, 2007). The largest percentage of unemployed persons during this period was therefore those between the fifteen to nineteen years category.   However, the legal age for employment in Trinidad and Tobago is eighteen years. Among this fifteen to nineteen years category of youth are usually those who   are out of school and present some form of delinquent behaviors.

(Downes 1999) noted that unemployment is particu-larly severe among the young population with the female rate much higher among poor families. He noted that poverty experienced by some individuals can be related to the labor market. He also noted that the education back-ground and attainment are important factors in the poverty labor market. It is therefore evident that unemployment has both social and economic implications for young persons. Many young girls are forced into prostitution as they struggle to support their families and often become exposed to HIV/AIDS. Some young men become involved in drugs as a means of earning an income and yet others become engaged in crime.

Youths are also socially excluded due to their poor economic situation. (Barker 2005) noted that no matter how poor one may be, they want to be part of the 'global-ized youth culture', this simply means that they need to fit in with what is happening with youth worldwide, where they can wear a brand name 'T' shirt or shoes. He noted that the media, particularly the television keep youth informed with the current fashion trends and many youth in turn attempt to keep abreast of them. They experience pressure and stress when they are unable to be part of the culture. However, for youth in difficult circumstances in Trinidad, the question of brand name is not the main issue. For these youth, fulfilling basic needs is quite challenging. It is therefore not a matter of choice of clothing but of what clothing is accessible to them. These youth are excluded from the mainstream and find other means of fitting in. The young men vent their frustration through violence, or gravitate towards a peer group that encourages violence. For them, manhood means earning an income, and becoming financially dependent to support themselves and their family. The inability to provide for themselves makes them "feel like a boy" and this strips them of their manhood.

(Deosaran 2007), in purporting the theory of "crime as rebellion," noted that it is not poverty that causes crime but rather the tensions emerging from the 'rich- poor gap'. He noted that youth incarcerated in juvenile homes are usually from poor, single – parent and low achievers. This statement emphasizes the point that no single factor is responsible for youth delinquent behavior, but rather a combination of factors. A poor economic condition, by itself therefore, will not be the only factor that influences the behavior of a child but rather a combination of other social factors.

Migration

Migration is a direct result of poor economic situations. A family in poor situations often has to migrate, looking for viable jobs to sustain the remaining members. They often leave children with grandparents, older siblings or friends while they seek a better life style. This arrangement allows some financial relief; however, it causes psychological harm to the remaining family members as they are often deprived of emotional support. The bonding that has taken place during the years is suddenly threatened as parents migrate, giving rise to the "barrel children" phenomena. It seems impossible to escape from the web of family ties, no matter how negative or positive the relationships have been. Some youth are exposed to all forms of abuse in their homes, yet if their families are in trouble they are protected by these children. They are affected by separation; however, they feel comforted when reunited. They are physically and emotionally abused yet they long for love from these abusers.

Research has shown that there are strong continuities from the quality of attachment in infancy to the handling of relationships in later life. It does not matter what children experience in their home, they long for the attachment and relationship of family members. (Varma 1997) concluded that family stability is an important aspect of maintaining secure families. The desire to fulfill the need to be cared for and protected leads a number of youths to join gangs where they can find this attachment.

An economic downturn in Trinidad and Tobago, during the late 80's and early 90's, caused families in the lower socio- economic categories to struggle to meet basic needs. This gave rise to adults migrating in order to improve their economic conditions. This contributed to an increase in sibling and single parenting (Sharpe & Bishop 1993). More recently, there has been a trend of female migrants. This affected the stability of families, particularly as the woman has carried out the role of the nurturer in the family. The impact of mother- separation often results in youth shifting homes, moving to unfriendly environments and lacking proper guidance.

A number of research studies indicate that family instability can augur negative influences that often lead to violence among young people. According to (Holder Dolly and Sogren 2004) children who witness violence in their environment were more vulnerable to family dysfunction and commonly experience behavioral, emotional and educational difficulties. This suggests that youth are exposed to unstable, unpredictable and potentially dangerous environments, which in many cases drive them to risky activities as a means of managing their challenges. This view was further supported by (Jones and Padmore 2004) who noted that such youth are likely to be exposed to economic exploitation, drug trafficking and are involved in higher levels of crime and drug use. The need to deal with their feelings of abandonment often propels them into situations of violence and crime.

(Bowlby 1961) posits that when children lose the parental relationship, they experience anxiety and loneliness which evokes a response that could range from depression to anger and hostility. He further identified stages they undergo such as anger, weeping, despair and finally development of a new interactive structure through which they can relate with their environment. Children of migrated parents are usually placed in extended families or with friends of their own family. In extended families, grandparents are faced with the responsibility to care for younger ones. However, being occupied with their affairs they often have little energy and time to supervise their grandchildren. Little attention is paid to the type of friends they keep or the activities in which they engage. When youth are placed with friends they usually have to make major adjustments to fit into the new family. However, when these youth become uncontrollable they are placed in institutions. These institutions provide care and protection, but the nurturing and emotional support is absent. These institutions also present another dilemma as children may often be verbally, sexually and emotionally abused. Having no recourse, the youth may runaway or become abusers themselves. The social implications for these children of migrated families are tough.

Abuse

The (British Association of Social Workers 1988) posits that child abuse represents a breakdown in the family system and a manifestation of a serious malfunction in the relationship between parents and children. Personal characteristics, environmental circumstances and stressful experiences of family members further exasperate the situation. They noted that it is important to understand the child, their family and the context in which the abuse has occurred. In Trinidad and Tobago and some Caribbean countries physical abuse may be a method used by parents to discipline their children. This method in most cases is learned behavior and parents are really socialized to behave in this manner. The practice of physical abuse Barrow noted may be an integral part of the family values, norms and practices. To the parent, this practice is effective parenting and not abuse. According to (Barrow 2001), child physical abuse in the Caribbean may be the result of normal behaviors which parents socially and culturally condone. It may then be viewed by the parent as an act of love and caring rather than a family dysfunction. To the child, the act may be viewed as abuse.

Child abuse constitutes all forms of physical, emotional, sexual abuse or exploitation, resulting in actual or potential harm to the child. Neglect on the other hand is the failure to provide for the development of the child in all spheres, whether it is health, education, emotional development, nutrition, shelter, or safe living conditions. This includes the failure to properly supervise and protect children from harm. As previously mentioned children in difficult circumstances usually come from poor families who are unable to provide basic needs. For these parents, the inability to provide safe living conditions, health care or proper education is no fault of theirs. They struggle to provide the basic necessities and in many cases depend on the young child to help them provide these needs. So, at an early age we find young children working in homes and factories, which constitute another type of abuse known as child labor. The situation of these youth and their parents is unavoidable unless support systems are put in place to help these families in difficulties.

Children in difficult circumstances are at high risk of sexual abuse. Although most sexual abuse is committed by family members or persons known to the abusers, children who live on the streets rarely know their perpetrators. (Marshall 2003) noted that these children spend most of their time on the street and find shelter in the night. These youths are usually uneducated as they leave school to provide for their families. They become vulnerable to street crime and sexual exploitation as they accept any offer that would provide them with basic amenities.

(Marshall 2003) further posits this view describing this category of youth as "Youth in the Street". He argues that parents see their offspring as a means of making money for them. He noted that these youths form groups where they can recognize common plight of social and economic abandonment and where they provide emotional comfort to each other. The literature strongly suggests that this social support is not without risk, prostitution, violence and exploitation. The dilemma faced by such youth is over-whelming and conditions in which they exist are deleterious. Abuse among families has also been a major concern in our society. (Holder Dolly and Sogren 2004) indicate that children show signs of trauma after being repeat-edly exposed to violent acts in their homes. The research indicates that children play various roles when exposed to violence, some cry for fear, some hide from the abuse, and some participate in the abuse in an attempt to protect the victim.

The research further indicates that many children have difficulty coping with feelings experienced during the trauma and may demonstrate some symptoms such as aggression," acting out", truancy and delinquency. Cognitively, it may be displayed through poor school performance; some of the females find themselves in homes of older men who offer them a 'better life' in exchange for sexual favors. The (Health

Economic Unit report 2005) indicates that in Tobago, the major channels of vulnerability were identified as domestic violence, sexual abuse and incest. The report suggests that females are most vulnerable to these dilemmas. According to (Sharpe and Bishop 1993), these youths often came from homes where the parents themselves were victims of abuse. These parents were also young and inexperienced therefore unable to cope with their own unmet needs and those of their children. The constant upheavals within the family have therefore been main indicators of difficult circumstances among our youth.

The literature suggests a number of conditions that lead youth in difficult circumstances to delinquent behaviors, namely poor economic situations, migration and family breakdown, labeling, unemployment and the prevalence of abuse. No one condition in isolation seemed to be responsible for the outcome of the youth, but rather, a combination of social conditions impact on the youth behavior. For instance, some youth may have grown up in poor economic conditions, yet, they have not turned to delinquency, while others who may be subject to poor economic conditions and little family support may engage in delinquent behaviors. The literature clearly shows that youth have been affected by poor economic situations which have emerged from an inadequate education system and the lack of job opportunities. The need therefore arises for youth consultation to ensure that programs identified are appropriate to youth development and empowerment.

The literature review also suggests that in order for young people to cope   with the difficult circumstances, they turn to peers who usually are in difficulty themselves. They seek economic support and are often lured into a company of lawbreakers leading them to a life of crime and violence. In addressing these situations some researchers noted that young people learn to cope by modeling their parents.

(Jones and Padmore 2004) noted that youth exposed to certain centers are more likely to act in that way. (Sharpe and Bishop 1993) expressed that their parents usually come from dysfunctional homes and inadequately address their difficulties. In addressing the difficulties, both (Barrow 2001), and (Sharpe and Bishop 1993) identified a holistic approach, recognizing that these difficulties do not lie with one system, but the impact of various systems.

While the body of literature seems to identify the problems youth in difficult circumstances face, not much have been able to provide viable strategies for addressing the specific categories. Youth continue to evade the programs designed for them. The real issues are that they yearn for love, attention and a relief of their economic situation. This research would add to the body of knowledge by firstly identifying the realities that cause youth to behave in a certain manner and secondly, by providing viable strategies that would assist youth as they attempt to manage these difficulties.

A significant weakness that was shown in the literature is the lack of attention given to the young female. This may be as a result of females being less visible on the streets as they are often enticed into homes of older men where they are given food and shelter in return for sex. The females therefore pose less of a threat to the increasing crime situation; however, their circumstances are as precarious as the male as they often find themselves in prostitution where they risk the chance of contracting HIV/AIDS and other sexually transmitted diseases. The literature, however, remains limited with respect to the consideration of effective intervention strategies for navigating these difficulties.

Although there are many policies that address youth development in Trinidad and Tobago, the proliferation of programs, the nature of youth issues, and the lack of systems to monitor and evaluate programs and policies make it difficult to assess the effectiveness of these efforts. Likewise, the fact that many youth in difficult circumstances are out of school, unattached to institutions, makes it an additional challenge to identify the nature of the problems faced by them and to design programs that meet their needs.

CHAPTER FIVE

Theoretical Framework/Methodology

In order to understand the context in which we address youth in difficulties, we must organize our thinking in a particular way; this is done through the use of theory. According to (Haralambos & Holborn 2004), theory is a set of ideas that provides an explanation for something. Though critics suggest that we should let the facts speak for themselves, the authors argue that there are no facts without theory.

This literature review identified a number of theories that can be used in addressing youth in difficult circumstances; however, the research adopted the ecological system, as this approach relates to the various systems that impacted the youth and their behavior. (Payne 1997) purports that much of what happens to youth in difficult circumstances are shaped by the environment in which they live. This model sees youth as constantly adapting in an interchange with many different aspects of their environment. He noted that where they are able to develop through change and are supported in this by the environment, reciprocal adaptation exists. However, social problems such as poverty and stigma pollute the social environment reducing the possibility of reciprocal adaptation. They therefore need appropriate inputs such as basic needs and other resources to survive. (Payne 1997) The model also sees the problems youth face, arising from life transitions such as development change, role and status change, environmental pressures such as unresponsive organizations, and interpersonal processes, as exploitation and abuse.

The theory describes these influences as inter-cultural, community organizational and interpersonal (Bronfenbrenner 1979). Bronfenbrenner realized that not only the environment directly impacted the youth, but that there were layers in between, which all had resulting impacts on the other level. He considered the individual, the organization, community and culture to be the nested factors.

The ecological model perceives youth development taking place in overlapping interrelated spheres that include family, school and community. (Payne 1997) identified these as the underlying causes of their behavior, which he noted, stemmed from three levels: the macro- environment of the society, the micro environment of the family and the individual. The macro level refers to the institutions that affect the youth, but in which the youth has no direct contact. This includes the media, the institutional framework and the education system. The media plays an important role by teaching and influencing beliefs, values, behaviors and attitude. The institutional framework can influence the difficult circumstances youth face if it is corrupt, inefficient and unresponsive to the needs of youth. The education system, in particular can play an important role in the youth's life as it influences the norms and values learnt. The micro- level refers to those individuals and institutions that interact with the youth on a personal level, such as the structure and dynamics of the family, and the social influences of peer groups and the community in which they live.

These interpersonal attributes are strong and influences how an individual perceives oneself. Some of the qualities are learned in the group; however, many are ingrained through gender and ethnicity. In the interpersonal sphere, there are also many components of the individual which includes the physiological and cognitive. While the physiological determines health and growth of the youth, the cognitive determines how the youth assimilate information, interpret and use it. High self- esteem can be a positive factor for the youth in this case. The family in particular, is expected to play an important role as it provides psychological support, encouragement, love and acceptance. (Barrow 2001) The inability of the family to provide these needs has therefore contributed to the difficult circumstances the youth experience.

(Barrow 2001), in examining youth in difficult circumstances, also looked at the ecological model, which assumes that no one factor in isolation can explain the occurrence of abuse. Using this holistic approach assumes that much of youth crime has also been associated with socio-economic frustration. (Sharpe and Bishop 1993) supported this model by stating that problems of increasing crime among youth may have been alluded to factors, which historically and currently impact upon the process of social integration of large sectors of the youth population. The theory therefore examines the macro, the micro and the individual system and how they impact upon youth development and therefore provides a framework in which these can be addressed. The model considers the complex interplay between the individual relationship and community and social factors, therefore allowing us to address the factors that place people at risk of perpetrating and experiencing violence.

On the other hand, some sociologists view marginalization as a key contributor to deviant behaviors. Sociologists, in explaining opportunity structure theory, noted that in a society where culture stresses material success, but which offers only some members the means to pursue it, is a society in which one can expect deviance. The choice the individual makes, sociologists call adaptation (Neubeck and Glasberg 2005). A youth deprived of opportunities to achieve his goals may therefore chose to engage in different ways to achieve material success. The macro-level according to the ecological approach can influence the way in which individuals are treated and therefore be the cause of this marginalization.

(Varma 1997) in the study of Troubled Children and Adolescents posits that the cause of deviant behaviors is multi-factorial. Individuals inherit certain potentials such as aggression, however the extent to which they engage in these behaviors is determined by the environmental circumstances with which the person comes into contact. This theory also purports the view of the ecological model. Varma further states that when these inherited predispositions are overlaid with disadvantaged environmental circumstances such as poverty, violence, labeling, abuse and unemployment, deviant behaviors are likely to emerge.

Labeling was also identified in this review as a means of explaining the context in which the term deviant behaviors is exhibited. Determining a behavior as deviant is subjective and some sociologists refer to it as socially constructed. It is relative to time, place, and circumstances as what is considered deviant may change over time in a single culture or society or may differ between cultures at any single point in time. According to the ecological model, labeling can be seen as an influence from the macro and micro system and therefore impacts on the individual functioning. We therefore need to explore the social conditions in which the youth display this behavior before we label them as deviant.

In summary, the ecological model identified a number of conditions in which we can attribute to youth behavior. The model looked at the different systems that impacts on youth behavior, it also looked at labeling and marginalization as major contributors to youth behavior. The theoretical framework for this study was developed by focusing on the various systems that impacted on the youth performance and their development. The ecological model emerged as the most appropriate model as it provided a framework in which the researcher can relate to the experiences of youth as they interact with the various systems. The theory therefore advances a view that the youth is not solely responsible for the behaviors they display, but that each system has an important role in contributing to the values, morals, and the behaviors of young people.

Methodological Approach

In order to achieve the stated objectives, the following methodological procedures were employed. This study adopted a mixture of both quantitative and qualitative approach. The qualitative approach facilitated a comprehensive exploration of the youth problems in the environment. This includes the macro, which addressed the Government and Non- Government resources available to the youth. The micro which looked at support systems from the child's family and immediate environment and the individual which looked at problem solving skills utilized by the child.

Primary data were obtained through structured interviews with managers, directors of youth programs and the youths who were participants of the program. Interviews were also held with teachers, guidance officers and the school's Dean, all chosen from institutions in the East of Trinidad. This information gave insight to the background of the youth, typical behaviors and feelings of those who participated in the program and the structure of the programs. It also allowed the researcher to understand the nature of the school system and the support that were available to youth in difficult circumstances.

Case studies were conducted with male students, who attended a senior comprehensive school and a vocational school. Both schools were located in the East of Trinidad. The case study included the parents and caregivers of the youth.

Secondary data was obtained from local newspapers, books related to youth and delinquency and statistical data from the Central Statistical Office and the Police Crime Analysis Unit. It also consisted of research materials available from the University of the West Indies Library as well as documents such as policies from the Ministry of Sports and Youth Affairs, and Ministry of Education. The focus of the documentary study was youth in difficult circumstances in the Caribbean. Information was sought on Government and Non-Governmental youth programs in Trinidad that are available to youths in difficult circumstances. This back ground information helped form the literature review and provided justification for the study.

Research Design

A case study is a research method which involves in-depth, longitudinal examination of a single instance or case. It provides a systematic way of looking at events, collecting data, analyzing information, and reporting results. As a result the researcher will gain a deeper understanding of why the situation occurred and what might be important to study more extensively in future research (Flyvbjerg 2006) The case studies conducted in this research provided in-depth description of the youth and their family, the circumstances under which they exist, the characteristics of the people involved and the nature of the community in which they are located. The underlying assumption is that the case will take place in its natural setting while striving for a more holistic interpretation of the situation under study.

Structured interviews were used to gain specific information on the structure of the youth programs, their success and failure rate and its relevance to youth in difficult circumstances.

Selection Process

Case studies were selected since it has the potential of providing a more comprehensive picture and a deeper insight in the lives of the youth in difficult circumstances. The interviews with teachers, guidance officers and the school Dean were geared towards selection of the cases. Information- Oriented sampling was used to identify the individuals for the case study. This type of sampling is a method used where one can identify a specific case that has the characteristics of the topic under study, a critical case, in this instance, is youth in difficult circumstances. One of the institutions chosen was a vocational school; this institution provided the prototype for the research study as the youths who attended the institution fit one or more of the categories of youth in difficult circumstances. The other youths came from a senior comprehensive school. In this case, the guidance officer and teacher were asked to identify a youth who fits the category of youth in difficult circumstances. The definition of 'difficult circumstances' was explained to the teachers and guidance officers as described in the study. The youths chosen were males, who were in their late teens and were in their final year of school.

Data Collection

Data was collected from case studies. A questionnaire guide was designed for the discussion with the youths to ensure that pertinent questions were not omitted. Questions were mainly open- ended giving the youth the opportunity to share as much as they desired. Discussions were focused on three areas, one consisted of demographics such as age, religion and ethnicity, the other contained family structure and dynamics and the third addressed the difficulties participants faced and the problem solving skills employed. The discussions with caregivers and significant others were informal. In some cases participants used the information sharing session as a therapeutic session where they gave vent to their social and emotional issues. In such cases, the researcher provided the forum for venting while utilizing the information for the benefit of the study. In other cases, participants sought help in dealing with their social and financial situations. In such cases participants were referred to the relevant authorities for intervention. The interviews with program directors were focused on the structure of the programs.

Procedures

In an effort to reach the stated objectives, the researcher had to undergo certain procedures.

- The guidance officer of the senior secondary school and the teacher of the vocational school were informed of the research and the need to conduct interviews. Specific terms were explained to them in order to ensure validity of the study.

- Students were chosen based on the informa- tion- oriented- selection procedure. Information –Oriented selection means that individuals were chosen based on their characteristics displayed as a youth in difficult circumstances.

- Participants chosen were informed of the topic area of the research and the anonymity and confidentiality as participants.

- Consent forms were distributed for participants consent in participating in the discussion.

- These forms introduced the researcher as a student of the University of the West Indies and explained the topic area of research.

- Information sharing sessions were conducted in the homes of the youth and their parents as the researcher felt the home environment would provide a more realistic view of the situation under study, this allowed observation of the dynamics that took place within the family and those of their neighbors during these sessions.

- The youth sessions were separate and apart from those discussions held with their parents. The sessions were held in the privacy of their homes.

- The parent and caregiver also shared their information in a private room in the absence of their children.

- Likewise interviews with teachers and instructors were conducted in the school environment. Again the researcher was able to observe the dynamics within the school environment and in one case was able to see how the youth interacted with other peers.

- The researcher used the waiting periods both at the home and at the school to utilize her observational skills. These observations were recorded and included in the data collection.

- Interviews and discussions were taped, however, there were instances where participants did not want the discussions to be taped and their wishes were respected and adhered to. In such case, information was only written.

- In one case, a parent who was abused asked the researcher to stop taping the session so that she can describe her abusive situation. The participant desire was respected.

- Although the sessions were taped, the researcher took the time to record all information. This served as a backup system in case of any default with the taping and it also added to the reliability of the study.

- The duration of most of the discussions was approximately two hours. This was not because of the number of questions asked but due to the depth both parents and youth chose to engage.

- Sessions with Teachers, Dean and the Guidance Officer were much shorter in duration. Participants in these sessions were allowed to share what information they felt was relevant and what contributed to the youth performance.

- Apart from the verbal responses, the researcher was quite attentive to the participants' non verbal responses, this included body language and emotional contours. These observations were also recorded.

- On many occasions the nonverbal behaviors displayed indicated to the researcher that there was need to regress and review previous statements of the respondents.

- Nonverbal responses of parents were mostly emotional outburst, in the form of crying or expressions of giving up. These responses were in regard to their own abusive situations in which they lived and as a result of their inability to cope with their present situation. These observations were also recorded. Participants were referred to counseling in these cases.

- One youth displayed non-verbal responses such as unwillingness to sit in discussions for long periods. As the researcher observed these nonverbal signs, participants were given the option of continuing the sessions at another scheduled time.

- Another youth displayed signs of frustration of his present situation. These were observed through frowns and were clarified when specific questions were asked.

- Rephrasing and paraphrasing were also used. These measures insured accuracy of the contents.

- The data was taped and transferred to the researcher personal computer and then transcribed to a word document.

- Comparison was made with data taped and the data written to ensure reliability.

CHAPTER SIX

Data Analysis and Findings

Data Analysis

The data from this research was analyzed using content analysis. Content Analysis is defined by (Krippendorff 1980) as a research technique that involves specialized procedures for processing scientific data. Its purpose is to provide knowledge, new insights, a representation of facts and a practical guide to action. This approach clearly allows the researcher to accept unstructured symbolic communication as data and also allows the analyzing of unobserved phenomena regardless of whether language is involved.

Data for this research were transcribed and placed in categories. The first category was information sourced about the community in which the participants lived. This information was necessary to give the readers an insight on the history of the community, the geographic location and the culture of its present occupants. Other categories were drawn from trends seen in the data which were the observation of one or more variable at different times. For example, the two cases presented had incidents of abuse. Abuse was therefore presented as a category. Categories were built upon similarities, differences and unusual events. The researcher examined one case at a time and looked at both verbal and non verbal responses, examining the background of the participants and the influences that were present. Patterns of behavior, influences of systems and circumstances in which the youth lived provided the frame-work for analysis.

Validity and Reliability

Research is worthless without rigor; hence a great deal of attention was paid to reliability and validity in this research. The researcher therefore adopted several measures to ensure validity and reliability.

Triangulation was used in this study to enhance its rigor. This was done by using different methods in data collection to get a broader view of the subject under study. This involved interviews with various youth program managers, teachers, and Dean and guidance officers. Discussions were held with parents and caregivers of the youth and also the youth. This approach provided rich substance for the paper.

Ethical Considerations

Clarity of Study

Participants were explained the content and purpose of the study.

Benefits and Risk

Difficult circumstances

They were also informed of the risk involved and the process of referral to counseling if the discussions became too emotional.

Volunteerism

Participants were also informed that the process was voluntary and that they were free to terminate the process at any time.

Consent

Participants were asked to sign consent forms stating that they read and understood the contents and were willing to participate in the discussions and interviews. Permission was sought from the parents and teachers of the minor in the interview for them to participate in the study.

Anonymity

The type of school and the geographic location was identified, however both the names of the schools and the identity of all participants was withheld.

Confidentiality

The data obtaining names and contact numbers of participants were kept in a safe place in the home of the researcher and was destroyed at the end of the report.

All participants shared information in the privacy of their homes or schools where necessary. The computer and tape in which the confidential data was stored was accessible only by the researcher.

Limitations of the Research

- The process of acquiring data was not always without challenges as the researcher often encountered difficulties that required patience and use of skill.

- Most of the information sharing sessions required at least two hours and this was sometimes difficult to acquire from the youth. In one case the researcher   took two sessions to complete the discussions.

- Information sharing sessions began at the end of Christmas and it was difficult to meet with some of the participants since this period was also the beginning of the carnival season. Some participants were therefore busy preparing for the National Panorama competition while others were busy attending fetes. This meant making several visits to the home to meet with them.

- During the interview the guidance officer and the teacher was preoccupied with the number of incidences taking place in the school at that time. While they were willing to accommodate the researcher, they found themselves occupied in addressing the affairs of other children.

- During one of the discussions, the participant who was pregnant was experiencing discomfort due to her pregnancy; this made the researcher feel very uncomfortable.

Research Findings

This section gives a descriptive report of two case studies consisting of nine individuals in east of Trinidad. It also consists of data accumulated from the school Dean, teachers, and the guidance officer. It includes basic data on the community in which the youth lives, an in-depth study of the youth, and their families and the circumstances in which they live. Results are presented under the following subheadings:

Community Profile

Demographics

Home Environment

Abusive Situations

Support Systems

Academic Performance

<u>Discipline</u>

<u>Problem Solving Skills</u>

Community Profile

The researcher believes it is important for the readers to get an historical and cultural perspectives of the geographic location in which the participants of this research live. It is believed that the environment in which an individual lives, impacts on the way the individual behaves. The culture of this community informs the behaviors of people, their thoughts and perception. Individuals who are not originally from that particular community usually behave differently and are seen as deviants when they do not conform to the norms and values of the original descendants. This perception formed by descendants usually impacts on the way in which people within the community interact with each other and would therefore impact on the behavior of its members.

Arima is located in the East of Trinidad, it extends to the eastern coast and includes Matura, Manzanilla, to the Arouca River on the West, Upper and lower Caroni to the south and to the southern foothills of the northern range. As of the year 2000, the Central Statistical Office report noted that Arima consisted of 28,310 persons, thirty percent of whom attended school while the remaining seventy percent did not attend school. The data indicated that about thirty percent of the occupants were not of school age, forty percent were under the age of forty and that the majority of its dwellers were Catholics.

The name Arima preserves the memory of its earliest pre-Columbian inhabitants. The town and parish of Arima came into existence when the Catholic mission was founded in 1785. In the mid 19th century it was the largest and most catholic parish in the diocese of Trinidad. The first people who lived in Arima were the Carib-Ameridians called Arimagotos. They had dominated the cocoa industry in 1876. By late nineteenth century, considerable social change had taken place, there was an influx of new residents and other religions were slowly making their appearance. However, the Catholics, because of their wealth, managed to maintain an overwhelming majority. This process of change was also reflected in the language, as the Spanish dominated town had been whittled away by French patois and eventually English.

The community strongly depended on the church, as the parish priest often provided the much needed financial support and was also the only barrier against them being evicted as squatters from their land. Drastic changes took place, and Arima no longer was an agricultural community with cocoa as its main crop. There was now a blend of races living together and the boundaries extended to areas which included Santa Rosa Heights, La Horquetta and Malabar. Few Africans went into business as East Indians and Syrians replaced the cocoa industry with jewelry stores and supermarkets. To date, the dominant religion in Arima remains catholic with a large percentage of Africans who replaced the mixed races. The income level and the educational level of these residents remained low and youths continue to be the dominant persons in the community. In spite of the influx of residents, Arima remains a cohesive community with strong ties to the Catholic Church. They continue to own businesses and control the wealth of the community. The new residents of Arima, due to the extensions of boundaries, continue to form their own community, expressing different norms and values from the original occupants. Their main form of communication is through business transaction.

Case One

Demographics

The youths and their family members were asked specific questions concerning their age, ethnicity and religion. They were also asked about their family composition as it is believed that the composition of the family impacts on the behavior patterns and their economic state.

The members of this family were of African descent and were Jehovah witnesses. The family consisted of six members, they included twin boys, who were fifteen years old, two older brothers in their middle twenty, and a sister sixteen years old and their sixty seven year old grandfather. The grandfather is a widower. The children previously grew up in a single parent home with the mother as the sole bread- winner. However, their mother died recently leaving the children in the care of their father. One of the older brothers is married and moved with his wife away from the other siblings. The other brother lived with the grandfather, but had to leave the home since he smokes marijuana and is often in conflict with his grandfather. The grandfather took over the responsibility of caring for the three younger children after they were taken from their father and placed in a children's' home. The existing family now consists of the twins, and their grandfather. They presently live in a two bedroom apartment in Arima. While the grand-father lived in Arima for a number of years, the children had recently moved in with him. The participant in this study was one of the twins; however, in describing the story I often refer to the two children as they were always together and looked identical. In addition, they shared similar experiences. However, when the participant experiences were different I referred to the participant as an individual.

Home Experiences

The children attended the Jehovah Witness assembly with their grandfather at least twice a week. Though the family did not share many experiences together, attendance at the assembly was mandatory and they were punished if they did not attend. The neighbors did not relate with the children as the children were accused of stealing cell phones from their peers in the neighborhood. One neighbor allowed the twins to sleep in her garage whenever they were locked out of their home. The grandfather maintained a good relationship with the neighbor in spite of the labels neighbors attached to his grandchildren. The relationship with the grandfather and the children was strained as the children hardly spent time at home. They attended school and in the afternoon spent most of the time walking the street. They will often return late at nights. The grand-daughter attended a vocational school, but became pregnant and had to drop out of school. She spent most of her time at her home or at the home of her boyfriend's parents. Her child's father lived abroad and was not in a position to support the child.

The environment in which the family lives is one surrounded by many young people who are gang members. The neighborhood youths are   involved in stealing and there are gang fights in the community. There is one neighbor who lives two streets from this family and who would lend support to the participant, yet he was not allowed in her house as he was labeled the neighborhood thief.

Abusive Situations

Abuse in this family began when the mother of these children was a teenager. As a teenager, she experienced physical and sexual abuse from both family members and strangers. At the age of fifteen she had her first baby and in an effort to support the child, she formed relationships with other men. Her five children had three different fathers, but no consistent provider, thus she was forced to find other partners who would give her money in return for sex. During this period she contracted HIV/ AIDS and died as a result. Her life according to her father was that of a street girl. She was physically abused on many occasions by her partners and he stated, "I often told her to come back home, but she never listened." Apart from the domestic work she did, her means of survival meant being on the streets. When she died the children were living with her common law husband, however, he use to sexually abuse his daughter and physically and emotionally abused the boys. He presently has a court case for this matter. Consequently, the children had to be taken away from him and placed in a Children's Home. The grandfather, believing that the care of the children was his responsibility decided to take legal custody of the children. The daughter lived a promiscuous life after leaving her father and became pregnant for a young man in the community, but by the time she had the baby, the boy's parents sent him abroad to live.

Support Systems

There was little financial support available to this family. The grandfather barely survived on his pension and National Insurance Benefits. The father of the girl no longer contributed to his daughter's welfare. The fathers of the other three children were not known by the grandfather. Members of the Jehovah Witness Assembly provided moral support and 'second hand' clothing for the children. The older brothers were not in a position to give financial assistance. The grandfather utilized his benefits to purchase his medication, pay bills   and provide financial support to the three children. He revealed that he had to give the boys twenty dollars a day for transportation and also find money for school outings. They received no spending money as he could not afford this. The twins often did evening jobs in the community to help meet their needs. Some of the jobs entailed working in the hardware and doing errands in the community. When asked what kind of errands, the participant hesitated and then informed the researcher that he cannot say.

The needs of this youth were as basic as providing meals and purchasing books for school. When asked about the school box lunch, he noted that it was a culture of the children in his school not to eat box lunch; if he eats it he will be heckled and mocked. He therefore preferred to stay hungry or steal food. When asked about the free school transport he noted that, although free school transport is available, he often had to negotiate his transport with the driver since the school maxi drivers reserved seats for their favorites, most of which were the school girls. The money the grandfather receives can barely meet the children schooling expenses. For him, parenting is a challenge. He noted;

> God made mothers and fathers to take care of children - not grandfathers. I am not able to care for these children and they are aware of that so they do what they want. I feel they will kill me.

Academic Qualification

The members of this family had very little formal education. They all achieved primary level education but never completed secondary school. The mother never attended secondary school and the granddaughter had to leave vocational school in her first year due to her pregnancy. The grandfather was a skilled plumber and worked with the Government before he retired. His only training received was in plumbing. One of the older sons worked in a construction firm with no specific skill and the other brother left primary school and made no attempts to further his education. The twins were still attending vocational school in Arima. They were completing the adolescent development program. The participant's grandfather was seeking help for his grand sons as he felt he did not know what they will do after leaving school. When asked what he wanted to do after school, the participant noted; "I do not know, maybe I will work in the hardware." This participant admitted that he knew nothing of the youth programs available.

Forms of Discipline

Discipline was the only form of control the grandfather felt he had over the children. Unfortunately, this did not prevent them from engaging in behaviors of which he did not approve. The boys were locked out of the house when they came home late or if they did not attend religious meetings. When this happened, they would sleep in the neighbor's garage. When they returned home the grandfather will send them back where they spent the night. The girl was hardly punished as she had a young baby. The older brothers who sometimes visited the family would beat the boys whenever the grandfather complained about them. The boys felt that they were abused by their bigger brothers and believed that they could do nothing about it. Suspension was used as a form of discipline when the participant broke school rules. On one occasion when the participant stole money from the school, the grandfather had to repay the money to avoid the police getting involved.

Problem Solving Skills

The twins attended a vocational school as they were not successful in the common entrance examination. However, the participant was not applying himself to his school work and the teacher reported that he was very playful. He made fun of every-one in the class and did not take school work conscientiously. He often stole items from the school's kitchen, this included packs of orange juice, snacks and on one occasion he stole over three hundred dollars from the school. When asked about the incidence, he recalled that he was hungry and stole the snacks and the juice as he wanted something to eat. He recounted that the money was used to help buy clothes as he often received, "second hand' clothes from other people. He also felt that he had to assist his grandfather in maintaining the home so he did jobs in the community and stole items when he did not get money. He admitted to having a girl friend. She was the only person he shared his painful experiences with. She would usually listen to him and they will both cry about the situation. On many occasions they would have sex. His grand- father stated that when he goes to wash his grandson clothes, he would find condoms in the pocket.

Case Two

Demographics

This family was of African descent and was of a Muslim background. There were six members in this family. They consisted of a grandfather whose age was not revealed, a mother in her middle thirties, a step father who was in his late forties and three children The girl was twenty years old. One of the boys, a participant in the research, was seven-teen years old and his other brother, fifteen years old. The family lived in a two bedroom house owned by the grand-father who was incapacitated. They lived in Arima and the participant attended school in Arima. However, the family was originally from the West of Trinidad and recently moved to Arima.

Home Experiences

The grandfather occupied one of the bedrooms, the brothers and sisters occupied the second bedroom and the mother and stepfather slept on the couch in the living room. The relationship with the child and his mother is strained; however he claims to have a good relationship with his father. The three children have three different fathers. The participant will normally spend time by his father. His stepfather who lives in the house seems to have a good relationship with the participant; however, the stepfather spends most of his time at home drinking and smoking. His elder sister spends most of her time away from home. When she is at home she relates to her brother only by using abusive language. The younger brother spends most of his time with his peers in the community. The mother is presently pregnant for the man she lives with. This man moved in the house six months ago when the mother moved in to live with her father. Prior to this, she lived on the streets and at homes of men she had relationships with. The neighbors speak to the family; however, they seemed to be a disturbed community as neighbors used obscene language to their own children and other members of the community.

Abusive Situation

The mother of these children, at the age of eight years, was sent to live at her father's home because her mother could not support her financially. During her stay with her father he physically abused her and at the age of thirteen years he put her on the streets to live. As she wept she stated:

> My mother did not want me and dropped me by my father at the age of eight years. My father could not handle me and put me out at the age of thirteen years. Imagine - I lived on the streets close to his home and he did not even take me back.

She lived on the streets working in night clubs trying to make a living. She was raped by a stranger and had her first child who is now twenty years. Looking for help to care for this child she got involved in an abusive relationship and had her second son. The intensity of the physical abuse led her to run away and she returned to the streets with her two children. She found another man who treated her kindly and took her to his home. She became pregnant for him with her last son and he soon began physically abusing her.

The participant was not happy as he saw his mother being physically abused every day. If she looked out the window and another man talked to her she would be physically abused. The participant, though he was not a recipient of the abuse at home, witnessed abuse all his life. Relief came to his mother when her father became blind. She volunteered to stay in his home and take care of him. She left that abusive relationship and took her children to her father's home. She met another man who she claimed loved her and treated her well. She then brought him into the home to live with them. The participant of this research is very angry with men as he claims that all of them beat his mother. At school, he is teased and physically abused by his peers. They find him to be quiet and they take advantage of him because of this. Since he has very little friends he spends most of his time liming with these very abusive peers. However, he attempts to fight them in self-defense.

Support Systems

The mother received welfare to assist the family but complained that since she moved to her father house she stopped receiving any welfare. She occupied herself in domestic work, but had to discontinue since she has to care for her father and she is also expecting a baby. Her eldest daughter is employed in a clothing store and the little money she receives is spent on transportation and clothing herself. The grandfather who is incapacitated is a recipient of welfare benefits. The step- father is employed occasionally as a taxi driver when his friend vehicle is available. There is no other support offered to this family. Their neighbors seem to be in their own predicament and cannot afford to offer help. The participant works on weekends and holidays to buy any books needed, clothes and pay transportation. When he visits his father he sometimes gets twenty dollars. His mother expresses no love to him and he often feels unwanted. He divulged that on many occasions he will go on the streets and cry. He has one male friend around his age in whom he will confide. His favorite teacher listens to him, but he cannot share all his secrets with her as the other teachers will hear about it. He confessed that he likes his Guidance Officer, but she spends little time with him.

Academic Qualification

The participant did not know or did not want to reveal his parents' educational status or occupation. However in speaking to the mother, it was realized that she did not attend secondary school. The sister attended secondary school, but left in form three. The other brother was enrolled in a secondary school but hardly attended and the participant was in form five of a secondary school, and now preparing for final examinations. His teachers complained that he missed too many classes and when he is present at school he goes behind the school to drink alcohol. They do not believe he will do well and often tell him so. The Dean of the school stated that the participant will not make it academically and was just wasting the Government money. However, his mother is of the opinion that he will do well in school if he stopped following bad company. This participant feels that he is doing well, but does not have any plans for his future. When asked about the Government after school youth programs. He said he was not interested, though he did not seem to be aware of them.

Forms of Discipline

The participant receives punishment from his mother when she gets angry with him. She would deprive him of going on outings with his peers. His mother becomes concerned when he is out late at nights, but because she is pregnant, she tries not to worry too much. She claims that she is fed up scolding him and does not know what she can do to curb his behavior. She quarrels with him most times and calls him abusive names. In school, the social worker is over burdened with other children and hardly finds time to talk to him. She is aware of his social condition since he is suspended from school very often. However, she noted that unless a child is referred to her by the principal or the Dean she cannot intervene. This child has not yet been referred, however, he has been suspended from school on many occasions. During the period of the interview this participant was suspended for drinking alcohol on the school compound.

Problem- Solving Skills

The participant noted that he drinks alcohol when he is stressed with his situation at home. He spends little time at home as a result of this and he is always on the streets. He finds himself among the very gangs which tease him since these are his only companions. Interestingly, occasionally they may protect him from others. On the other hand, he knows he cannot trust his companions completely. On one occasion, he was liming in Arima when he was accused of stealing a cell phone and was arrested. The matter is presently before the court but he believed he was framed by his peers. He claims that when his mother denies him the privilege of going out with his friends he would leave home on the pretense of going to school and stay away from home for three days. When asked where he spends his days he says he goes to his fathers' home. His mother gets angry about this because she claims that the father does not support the child financially but always wants the child to help him do work at his home.

CHAPTER SEVEN

Interpretation of Data and Summary

In the two cases presented, the families had been experiencing extreme difficulties and the participants can be referred to as youths in difficult circumstances. They live in unfriendly environments where neighbors are always in conflict. The stress within the family tends to perpetuate frustration among the young ones. The stigma attached to these young people has kept them from the support and guidance needed by older community members. Obtaining an education seems difficult to acquire as their poor social conditions has led them to engage in seeking employment. Based on the history of the community the present residents were mainly migrants to Arima and therefore did not foster a community spirit.

The culture of the community consequently provided a framework in which the residents behaved. Individuals who migrated to this community and did not conform to the expected behaviors were seen as outcast and delinquents and as a result were not accepted as part of the community. These migrating families were therefore ostracized and were not given any community support, their problems eventually became more than they can handle.

The youth in these cases had experiences of moving from one family to another, while their parents attempted to find stable homes. They experienced abuse as victims themselves and as witnesses to the abuse of their own family members. These experiences triggered angry feelings and feelings of neglect, hence they often left their family homes and found friends on the street.

The literature review spoke about many of these experiences of youth, as it alluded to the fact that the instability in families' auger negative influences which often leads to violence. They also divulged that when children lose parental relationship they become lonely and hostile to those they interact with. The two youths in these studies have little support systems and have faced a number of traumas in their lives. Their experiences are mainly responsible for the shaping of their thoughts and behaviors. Unless they are provided with the appropriate resources, love and care they need, they tend to be heading to a life of crime and violence.

Life for these parents has been traumatic, as they were often abused by men in their quest to obtain financial support. Not only were the parents affected by the abusive situations but it left emotional scars on the children who witnessed it. Many research studies alluded to the fact that abuse in the   life of a youth tends to shape their sense of self and identity and prohibits positive development even when opportunities for this development are present. When these experiences are combined with absent fathers and other interpersonal deprivation states, the youth becomes more highly vulnerable. Other Caribbean researchers noted that victims of abuse usually come from abusive homes and the difficulties they face cause them to display delinquent behaviors. They are also more likely to experience behavioral and educational difficulties. The cycle of abuse inevitably continues. These victims make several attempts to get out of their situation, but their circumstances overwhelm them and they return to their previous state.

These families seem to be lacking an effective social network. The neighbors are occupied with their own parenting challenges, there seems to be no assistance or connection with the extended family members apart from a grandparent who may be too ill or old to lend support. Neither of the family members seems to be aware of any formal social network apart from the welfare received from the Government.

The trend of grandfather parenting seems to be a new phenomenon in the Caribbean as fathers are frequently absent from the home and mothers are occupied trying to make a living either in Trinidad or abroad. In both instances either parent are away from their homes for long periods and leave their children in the hands of grandparents. In most cases the both grandparents will take the parenting role or in some cases the grandmother, it is exceptional when a grandfather takes that role. This is quite a challenge for him as the difficulty faced is not only to manage the financial aspect but to address the social issues that are presented on a day to day basis. More challenging is the changing dynamics in parenting our youth today, where parents have to be constantly in up to date with the trend of this new generation.

For youth in difficult circumstances, their reality is different in every dimension. They grow up in damaging family situations in which their basic needs are not met and the developmental foundation of childhood has been poorly laid or perhaps not at all there.

Young persons are influenced by the peer group more as a result of the parental disregard for them than their attractiveness to the peer group. The vacuum left by the withdrawal of parents and teachers from the lives of youths is often filled by this undesirable peer group. It is therefore important for both parents and teachers to take an active role in shaping the attitudes and behaviors of our youth. They need to take time to listen and understand the feelings of these young people so that they can take appropriate intervention strategies in assisting them.

Suspension is the main form of discipline in the school system. Startlingly, there are no follow up activities, no social work intervention; it provided no avenue for behavior change and no personal counseling. The youth is therefore left at home without supervision and exposed to the poisonous elements in the environment. This method of punishment may provide more harm than good to the child.

The situations presented in the two case studies provided the researcher with information to form a theo-retical base. While the researcher may assume that children learn most of their behaviors from their home environment, it should be noted that the peer group usually provide excel-lent opportunities for learning the social response to the difficulties they face.

The ecological model sees these youths behavior as being shaped by the environment in which they live. This environment constitutes the school, the home and the community. The family system and its experiences of poverty, abuse and strained relationships contributes to the shaping of behaviors and attitudes of the youth. The youth also learns how to behave and respond as they model the behavior of their parents. Their experiences of poverty deprive them of basic needs and place them in situations where they are stigmatized by their peers and other members of society. This includes the job market. The policies and programs available do not always appeal to the young people and as a consequence they abstain from participation. Trapped with life transitions such as, develop-ment changes, environmental pressures such as broken families, and poverty and their own interpersonal processes such as abuse and strained relationships, the youths struggle to maintain a good fit.

Summary of Findings

The difficulties youths face is undeniably a challenge for many of them. The family which is the main support system has

failed in providing the care, love and protection they need. The early experiences of these young people chart the path for their future. The inability to effectively manage these experiences results in serious social and economic consequences for the youth themselves and society at large. With little support received, when faced with these dilemmas, the youth turn to their peers where they can find solace. Their peers are often victims of the same difficult circumstances and often carve their own ways to alleviate their conditions. This research revealed that problems affecting youth were due to an inadequate support system, first at home and also in the secondary schools. The youth are often caught up in the role to provide for themselves and other siblings.

There also is evidence of a breakdown of effective family relationships; this includes the absence of fathers and their irresponsibility in supporting their offspring. Key issues that also arose out of this study were the need for youth in difficult circumstances to contribute to the family's income. These findings are consistent with the literature examined which suggests that youth faced with various difficulties, in an attempt to manage, turn to peers who usually have their own challenges, seeking both emotional and economical support. Often these youths are lured into company of law breakers leading them to a life of crime and delinquency.

The research also indicates that the school system provides inadequate support for youths in difficult circum-stances. These youths are confronted with dilemmas at home and often act out these experiences in the class room. However because of insufficient social support, such as social work intervention and psychosocial assessment, these students are further expatriated by being suspended from school. The period spent away from school without any focused intervention, leaves the student to fend on their own, often engaging in illegal activities. In both cases, the families were unable to manage without the intervention of the state. However, little intervention was received. These youths are still at the stage where intervention can help, nevertheless, if left much longer without structured intervention, society may regrettably pay the cost.

As future leaders, the wellbeing of our youths is critical. It is consequently necessary for policy makers to build on the available research and provide the necessary support and intervention needed for youth development in Trinidad and Tobago.

CHAPTER EIGHT

Conclusions and Recommendations

Presently as the researcher attempts to conclude this paper, the situation of crime and violence in schools persist. Within one week there have been reports of one teenager stabbing to death another school mate at a school in north Trinidad. It has been alleged by media reporters that the dispute was over forty dollars. Less than one week later teachers from another secondary school in the east of Trinidad walked out of the school compound for fear of their lives as a student attacked another student with a cutlass. The spate of crime both in the wider society and the school system is alarming. Definitely, the measures implemented are ineffective and barely makes a dent in providing viable solutions. We therefore must revise our present strategies and collaborate with researchers and policy makers to address the problems of youths in difficult circumstances.

The research paper identified a number of inadequacies in addressing youth in difficult circumstances both at the micro and macro level of society. These included the lack of proper role models to provide the guidance needed by youths, inadequate support systems within the school and home environment and the need to provide support and guidance to assist parents in performing their parental roles. In attempting to alleviate some of the difficulties faced by these youths, the researcher would conclude by making some recommendations for future empowerment and development.

Recommendations

The Implementation of a National Mentoring System

This study suggests the need for the implementation of a national mentoring program for youths in difficult circumstances. This program should be executed in collaboration with Government Organizations and the private sector. The program will facilitate youths who are unable to secure the right mentors to guide them through their various transitions. The researcher suggests that this must be a highly structured program since the identification of proper role models have proved challenging. One must consequently apply a rigid selection process in securing a mentor. This program can also provide dual mentor relationships where youths can benefit from the learning experiences of both male and female role models. This concept is to provide the youth with an adult who can act as a friend, a confidant and a role model.

The Deployment of a Social Support Team in Secondary Schools

There is also an urgent need for a social support team to be deployed in secondary schools. This team should comprise of the guidance officer who will give direction in terms of career choices, a social worker who will make social assessments and provide social work intervention for the youth and his or her family. This intervention will include referrals to other social agencies. It is also important to employ an education specialist who will make assessment on the child's capacity to cope with the scope of academic work presented and therefore channel the child through other avenues. This program would provide support to the students and also to their parents . Assessment can be made on their home situation and appropriate intervention can be made. This would alleviate the number of family concerns students bring with them in the school.

The Establishment of Correctional Schools

Correctional schools should be implemented to address the vast number of children who are suspended as a disciplinary action. This school should support youths on disciplinary charges by providing workshops on anger management, conflict resolution and other suitable life skills. This approach would avoid youths from liming on the streets during their suspended period and will provide them with opportunities of correcting their deviant behavior. The program for each individual should be the length of their suspension and should also include training in areas of drug abuse and effective communication.

The Implementation of a National Parenting Program

In some instances youths are parented by young adults due to the unavailability of legal guardian or the lack of physical ability of the grandparents to cope with them. These young adults are mainly an elder brother or sister who may not be equipped with parenting skills. The grandparent may also not be physically able or psychologically ready to deal with the changing dynamics of our modern day youth.

- It is then necessary for the Government to implement a national parenting program to provide these skills for all parents.

- In addition to these skills training there should be a support mechanism to help these parents who are experiencing financial difficulty. It is important to note that the skills training must be supported with financial assistance since many parents are unable to manage the little finances they receive.

The Development and Execution of Legal Measures to make parents accountable

The research further indicates that effective parental relationship has been lost. This problem can be addressed to some extent in the national parenting program, but there is need to institute additional measures to ensure that parents take responsibility for their parenting role.

- As such Government should put measures in place to make parents accountable for their children. This can be established through the development and implementation of legal measures. Incentives should be put in place to ensure that parents take responsibility for their children. This should start in the school system where parents take responsibility for their children's regularity, punctuality, and the completion of homework. Fathers must also be held accountable for their children's behavior. The researcher found it necessary to single out   fathers as the study revealed that fathers were absent from the home and did not take responsibility for their child.

The Restructuring of the Education System to Facilitate to Youths who must work to support their Families

The poor economic conditions of youths in difficult circumstances have caused many young people to seek employment to alleviate their poor conditions. Discouraged by their bleak job prospect, some turn to criminal activity such as sex and drugs to survive. While the researcher believes it is the responsibility of the parents to provide for their children, the reality is that this is not always the case. We therefore must provide legal options for our youth to obtain stipend while acquiring their skills.

- Provision should be made in the restructuring of the education system to facilitate youths who unavoidably must work and attend school. While it is the responsibility of parents to provide for their children, consideration should be made to youths who live on their own and the single parent who really cannot afford to provide basic amenities for their families.

- The availability of a formal structure to suit the needs of these youths would avoid the need for youths to participate in the illegal job market.

- Consideration should be made to youths who learn a trade in secondary schools, where these youths can practice on clients for a small fee. This can be in areas such as gardening and hairdressing.

A major concern for policy makers would therefore be an effective education system with structured programs that cater to the varying needs of youths in difficult circumstances.

Marketing of Social Programs within Poor Communities

Many of the social programs available to youths are not marketed within the communities. These programs are advertised in the newspapers, on television and markets where youths do not permeate. It is therefore our responsibility to have these programs advertised within the communities, with information officers available to give guidance as to benefits, access and knowledge of filling the application forms and participating in the program.

The application forms should be made available through community centers, health centers, youth groups and churches where youths can have easy access.

Strengthen Community Support

Government should provide incentives to community based innovative youth programs. These community based programs may be more sensitive to the needs of the youths in their community. Grants and subventions should be made available to innovative community projects that targets youth.

The Establishment of a Transitional Home

The many problems facing our youth are challenging, the intervention must be multifaceted. For many youths, facing the same community after a rehabilitation program can be disastrous. While their training in rehabilitation will prepare them for exposure with the negative elements, they may not be quite prepared for personal interaction with these negative elements. We must therefore provide alternative solutions to help them move forward. It is with this view, I strongly recommend a transitional home for those youths who live on the street because of abusive situations at home and for those who are discharged from various residential institutions and are unable able to find a home.

CHAPTER NINE

An Established National Program

A Firm Recommendation

It is a firm recommendation of this book that leaders of government entities should consider an established national program to mentor at-risk youth. Although, many productive mentoring programs are operated by faith-based, non-profit entities, NGO's, and private organizations, it remains necessary that a National Policy be produced to provide guidelines for operations and criteria for evaluation of mentoring programs. This is especially true since youth mentoring programs target individuals with already identifiable difficulties. This means that these at-risk young people are also at-risk to be exploited. For these reasons, plus the many positive results of mentoring, this author recommends established national mentoring efforts.

A National Response

As a writer and functioning professional in the field of mentoring, this author was able to assist the Government of Trinidad and Tobago in formulating a national policy for a mentoring endeavor. The Ministry of National Security, in the quest to promote positive youth development, has embarked on a National Structured Mentorship Program. This endeavor was designed to provide support to youths in difficult circumstances by pairing them with role models and teaching them fundamental life skills, civic responsibility and positive ways of relating to their peers.

Who Is A Mentor?

Think back to when you were growing up. Was there someone, other than your parents - maybe a neighbor, a family friend, an aunt or uncle, a coach - who shared time with you and made you feel special?

Being a mentor is about having fun. It's about sharing time and exploring the world together. A mentor provides inspiration, acceptance, challenge, a sympathetic ear and exposure to new ideas and activities.

It's about sharing little moments to create big magic!

Mentors are not:

- Substitutes for parents or teachers

- Providers of basic necessities like food and money

Your Role as a Mentor:

- Build a special friendship with a young person and have fun together

- Take the lead in establishing the friendship

- Talk, listen, support, guide, encourage - believe in them and help them believe in themselves

- Keep others informed about what you're doing. In most of our programs, you communicate directly with the families involved and our staff

- Keep in touch with your Mentoring Coordinator and ask questions you might have. We also enjoy hearing about the fun you've been having.

Our Role:

- Be there for you

- Assign a Mentoring Coordinator to you

- Do our best to match you with a young person who shares your interests, location and schedule

- Help make your match successful

- Cheer you on and help you out if you need it!

Self-Esteem & Relationships

Self-esteem, simply defined, is the concept people have of themselves. It plays a vital role in relationships, because it impacts:

- Independence

- Self-value

- Assessment of how others view them

- Ability to realistically assess strengths and weaknesses

Low self-esteem generally results from having a negative self-image. High (healthy) self-esteem results from having a positive self-image. People with healthy self-esteem are often confident, sure of themselves, and highly motivated. Moreover, healthy self-esteem is a cornerstone to developing good relationships because it allows for a deeper connection with others.

Acceptance

The concept of "acceptance" is very important in any discussion of relationship and self-esteem. A critical component in creating healthy relationships is the ability to observe feelings without judgment. People who accept themselves as they are, not as others may want them to be, are generally healthier and more content.

It is important to have a realistic sense of strengths and weaknesses. While there is always room for improvement, being too self-critical is damaging. Change occurs over time, and it is important for people to allow themselves that time.

Understanding Relationships and the Source of Emotional Drama

It can be difficult to understand a person we are in relationship with especially when sometimes we don't even understand ourselves. Why do we feel good about ourselves one moment and bad another? Why does a person change their attitude towards us from one day to the next? Each human is a complex creature whose behavior is driven by emotion, beliefs, point of view, and how much coffee they had that morning .Combine that with another person who is driven by different emotions, beliefs, point of view, and how much they drank last night and we have an opportunity for emotional drama and chaos. Some call it a roller coaster of emotion while others are calling for relationship help.

A National Mentorship Program

An Operational Manual
For Mentoring Programs

Introduction

The focus of the Mentoring program varies from dropout prevention, to job training, school retention and attendance, literacy, community development as well as prevention of substance abuse, teen pregnancy and violence and crime.

Given the major demographics and economic shift and trends in society, that is, increase in single parenting, decrease in extended family networks, and technological innovations, it is clear that the family and the community, traditionally the providers of social capital, no longer is able to provide the necessary support for a growing percentage of the youth population. The program therefore acts as a support system to youths at risk of experiencing these challenges.

The program aims to develop one to one relationships focused on youth's social and academic development. One to One mentoring refers to the intention to provide personalized attention and care to the young persons who participate in the program. Critical to the success of the program is the ability to provide one mentor for a mentee. The mentor will therefore mentor one mentee except in extreme difficult cases. The mentor is both a friend and role model who supports and encourages the mentee in holistic development.

The program facilitator will develop the mentoring process and ongoing training and support will be provided. A monitoring and evaluation system will be established.

MISSION STATEMENT

The Mentoring Program is designed to empower youth to make positive life choices that enable them to maximize their full potential

VISION STATEMENT

It envisions a society in which every youth experiences nurturing one-to-one relationships and community support, which in turn allows them to develop into their full potential capable of making informed, responsible decisions.

The purpose of this manual is to provide a common framework, based on best practice principles to support and inform the design of the development of mentoring program.

The objectives of the manual are to:

- Emphasize that mentoring is a voluntary developed relationship and not an imposed process.

- Recognize mentoring as a valuable element of youth development.

- Establish that mentoring relationships are governed by existing policies on quality, equal opportunity, code of ethics and confidentiality

HISTORY OF MENTORING

When Odysseus, King of Ithaca, left for the Trojan Wars around 800 BC, he was faced with a problem; who would look after the royal household and groom his son, Telemachus, for the throne in his absence? Odysseus turned to his trusted companion to mentor his son. Much was expected of Telemachus and his mentor had to prepare him for many roles. Since then great men and women in the Bible have been used to mentor others. Elizabeth mentored Mary, drawing from her own experience. Jesus told his disciples to "follow me and I will make you fishers of men."

The term mentor has since become proverbial for a faithful and wise adviser, and effective mentoring is an important step in professional success. Ideally, mentoring is a two way, professional relationship that develops over time, with each person asking questions, finding answers and making choices.

The term and concept is widely used today both in a formal and informal setting to guide young people.

Code of Ethics for Mentoring

Mentor should be guided by the highest standard of ethical behavior. The following principles should guide the behavior of participants of the program.

- Mentor and mentee should respect each other's time and responsibility, ensuring not to make unreasonable demands on each other.

- Mentor and mentee should share the responsibility of avoiding the creation of dependency in the relationship.

- The mentor must work on the basis of confidentiality with the mentee.

- The mentor must respond to the mentee's developmental needs and not impose a personal agenda on him/her.

- The mentor should not intrude in any area the mentee wishes to keep private.

- The mentor must always be truthful, forthright and trustworthy in relationship with the mentee.

- The mentor must not engage in any activities that will cause physical or psychological harm.

- The mentor must always be a positive role model.

- The mentor must relinquish the position of mentor if the vision and goals of the mentee are not shared.

- The mentor must be non-judgmental.

What is Mentoring?

Mentoring is a particular kind of relationship in which a person with identified abilities or competencies enables another human being to develop his/her own abilities and talents. It is commonly used as a method of transferring specific skills, knowledge and norms to individuals as a component in youth development. Mentoring is positively perceived and is a sanctioned role for unrelated adults to play in the lives of youths. It contributes to greater civility and responsibility for strangers.

The Mentoring Program focuses on dropout prevention, job training, prevention of substance abuse, teen pregnancy, violence and crime. Besides personalized attention and care the program is intended to provide youths with another form of support and access to resources that they have been systematically denied.

What are the benefits of mentoring?

For a mentoring program to be successful all activities must be approached with the specific goals and objectives of the people involved. The benefits of a mentor include:

- Satisfaction of helping youth reach their goals.

- Increased social awareness, leadership skills and advocacy skills

- Increased self-confidence.

Recruitment Policy

The **Mentoring Program** will conduct ongoing recruitment activities for new mentors. As such an annual recruitment plan will be developed and will include recruitment goals, strategies to achieve those goals, and time line. The program management team will assume lead responsibility for the recruitment of new mentors. Other staff such as the secretariat and supervisory team will support in these activities as required.

Mentor Eligibility Requirements

- Must be at least twenty-one (21) years of age.

- Be willing to adhere to the **Mentoring Program** policies and procedures.

- Agree to at least one (1) year commitment to the program.

- Commit to spending a minimum of eight (8) hours a month with the mentee.

- Complete the screening procedure.

- Be willing to communicate with the mentee weekly.

- Agree to attend mentor training sessions.

- Have a clean criminal history.

- Not a user of illicit drugs.

- Not a user of alcohol or controlled substances in an excessive or inappropriate manner.

- Have never been accused, arrested or convicted of child abuse or molestation.

- Not have falsified information during the screening process.

- Must reside in the country in which the program was initiated.

- Be willing to communicate regularly with the program supervisor and discuss activities.

Mentee Eligibility

- Be a participant of the project.

- Be able to obtain parental/guardian permission for participation in the program.

- Commit to spending a minimum of eight (8) hours a month with mentor.

- Agree to attend mentee training as required.

- Be willing to communicate regularly with the program coordinator and discuss monthly meeting and activity information

Screening

It is the policy of **Institutional Mentoring Program** that all mentor applicants complete screening procedure. At minimum, the following screening procedures are required for mentors.

Mentor screening procedure

- Attend twenty (20) hours mentor training.

- Complete written application.

- Complete criminal and character check.

- Complete personal interview.

- Complete drug testing

The decision to accept an applicant into the program will be based upon a final assessment done by program staff at the completion of the screening procedure. Successful applicants will be informed in writing of their acceptance. Unsuccessful applicants will also be informed, however, no reason will be provided to the rejected applicant.

All applicants are expected to meet the eligibility criteria. However, extenuating circumstances may be reviewed at the discretion of the program management and acceptance may be allowed. These circumstances are expected to be rare. Documentation of the screening process must be maintained for each applicant and placed in confidential files.

Training

The Mentoring Program will conduct training sessions for all mentors and mentees for a minimum of twenty (20) hours initial training prior to being matched. The agenda will cover basic program guidelines, safety issues, including mandatory reporting and communication/relationship building skills. It is the responsibility of the program coordinator to plan and develop training sessions.

The mentor training workshop will include:

- Understanding adolescent development
- Diversity and cultural issues
- Dealing with Crisis in the relationship
- Addressing conflict within the relationship
- Ethical issues in mentoring
- Gender sensitization
- The man in the mirror/ Who am I?
- Volunteerism
- Stages of the Mentoring Relationship
- Communicating with your mentee

Matching

The program staff should use the guidelines outlined in the match procedure prior to creating a mentor/mentee match.

The program staff will determine the suitability based on the following criteria:

- Preference of mentor/mentee
- Similar gender/ethnicity
- Common interest
- Similar personalities

Matches must be either male adult to male youth or female adult to female youth. In the case of match difficulties, discord or concerns, appropriate discussion and intervention must be undertaken to improve or rectify problem areas.

Recognition Events

It should be the policy of the **Mentoring Program** that all participants- including mentors and mentees be recognized as important to the success of the mentoring program. Particular emphasis will be placed upon recognizing the mentors. It is the responsibility of the program management to plan and implement the following recognition activities:

- Host an annual recognition event, including selection of mentor and mentee of the year.

- Feature a mentor's, mentee's success story in the newsletter.

Record Keeping Policy

The process of mentoring applications and matching must be documented for each potential mentor and mentee in a case file. All records are to be kept confidential. Records of past applicants and participants will be maintained for a period of three (3) years after the close of the participation. After three (3) years the records should be shredded and discarded with approval from the management. The management team will keep the stringent records of all program activities. All files should be updated within an electronic database and/or hard copy filing system.

Confidentiality

The Mentoring Program has the responsibility to protect the confidentiality of its participants and their families.

With the exception of the limitations below, program staff will only share information about mentors, mentees and their families with other professional staff of **the Mentoring Program.** All prospective mentors, mentees and guardian should be informed of the scope and limitations of confidentiality by program staff. Additionally, mentors are required to keep information about their mentee and his/her family confidential. Records are considered property of **program**, not the staff and should not be available for review by mentors, mentee or parents.

Limits to Confidentiality

- Information from mentor's and mentee's records may be shared with individuals under the following conditions-

- Information may be gathered about program partici-pants and shared with other participants, individ-uals and organizations only upon permission of the mentors, mentees and their guardian

- Identifying information (including names, photo-graphs, video) of program participants may be used in publications or promotional materials only upon written consent of the mentor, mentee or guardian.

- Information may be provided to the court in the event of litigation or potential litigation involving the organization. Such information is considered privi-leged information and its confidentially is protected by law.

- Program staff members are mandatory reporters and as such must disclose information indicating that a mentor or mentee may be dangerous to or intends to harm himself/herself or others.

Violation of Confidentiality

A known violation of the agency policy on confidentiality by a program participant may result in a written warning or disciplinary action such as suspension or termination from the program.

Closure Policy

This element is usually brief in its development and implementation, but very important. Improper closure could make the mentee experience feelings of abandonment and betrayal. All mentors and mentees of **the program** must participate in closure procedure when their match ends. Closure is defined as the ending of a formal match relationship regardless of the circumstances of the match ending of whether they intend to have future contact informally beyond the match duration.

Closure can occur for any number of reasons including the contracted match duration has ended, participants do not want to continue the match, or an individual no longer meets the requirements for the program. Future contact will be at mutual and informal agreement of the mentor, mentee and guardian. If future contact is agreed upon, the **Mentoring Program** will not be responsible for monitoring and supporting the match after ending. The management will verbally and in writing inform all parties – mentor, mentee, and guardian – that the match has ended and that **the program** will not be liable for any incidences that occur after the match has closed.

Evaluation Policy

Evaluation will be a key component in measuring the success of the mentoring program and for making continuous improvement in the effectiveness and delivery of mentoring services. Evaluation data will be collected every six (6) months.

Match Support and Supervision

The mentoring staff (supervisory) shall make monthly phone calls or contacts with all parties to each match including mentor, mentee, parent/guardian. Staff must record for each month dates, times, sport, description of activities. Beyond monitoring the match relationship and activities, program staff must undertake other efforts that support participants such as regular group activities for matches, a formal support structure for mentors and attainment of admission to community events/activities.

Mandatory Reporting

Any staff, volunteers, or mentor accused of child abuse will be investigated by the organization.

Contact with mentees will be restricted or constrained and/or the person in question suspended from employment or program participation pending on the severity of the situation.

Unacceptable Behavior Policy

A number of behaviors are regarded as unacceptable with **the Mentoring Program** goals, values and standards and are therefore prohibited while participants are engaged in mentoring activities.

- Unwelcome physical contact such as inappropriate touching, patting, pinching and physical assault.

- Demeaning behavior of either a sexual or non sexual nature, including threats of such behavior.

- Display of suggestive or pornographic materials.

- Known sexual abuse or neglect of a child.

- Possession of illegal substances.

Any unacceptable behavior, as specified but not limited to the above, will result in a warning and/or disciplinary action including suspension or termination from partici-pating in the mentoring program.

Home Visits

It is the policy of the program to encourage mentor/mentee visits within their own community and limit over-night visits. However, home visits are permitted under the following conditions.

- It must be permitted only after six (6) months of the mentor/mentee relationship.

- Permission must be given by parents and manage-ment team.

- The nature of the visit, activity plan and purpose must be stated.

- Permission from the parent must be stated in writing.

- Mentor must provide the following information prior to the departure

- The destination

- Phone numbers

- Places to be visited

- Expected time of return

Procedures for Re-matching during the Program

If at any period during the mentoring process, a mentee has to be re-matched for any reason the following procedures must take place.

- The decision must be discussed with the mentee by a member of the supervisory or management team.

- The mentee must undergo counseling with the program psychologists/counselor.

- Both the psychologists/counselor and mentee must determine the mentee's state of readiness to enter another relationship with a mentor.

Recruitment Procedure

- All staff members must receive training on the principles of recruitment and are required to understand **the Mentoring Program** recruitment plan.

- The program coordinator will finalize and distribute the yearly recruitment activity plan to the staff.

- Based on the tracking data and overall effectiveness of the recruitment efforts, the coordinator will revise the strategy as needed.

- The coordinator will provide yearly plans for recruitment and marketing strategies.

- Recruitment exercise will be undertaken by the management staff under the direction of the program coordinator.

Mentor Job Description

The **Mentoring Program** helps to empower youths in our community to make positive life choices that will enable them to maximize their potential. The Mentoring Program uses adults to commit to supporting, guiding and being a friend to a young person for at least a period of one (1) year. By becoming part of the social network of adults and community members who care about youth, the mentor can help youth develop and reach positive goals.

Mentor's Role

- Serve as a positive role model and friend.

- Build the relationship by planning and participating in activities together.

- Strive for mutual respect.

- Build self-esteem and motivation.

- Help set goals and work toward accomplishing them.

Time Commitment

- Make at least one (1) year commitment.

- Spend a minimum of twenty (20) hours per month one to one with the mentee.

- Communicate with mentee weekly.

- Attend training sessions.

Requirements for Participation

- Willingness to work with young people.

- Willingness to adhere to program policies and procedures.

- Willing to complete application and screening process.

- Dependable and consistent in meeting time commitments.

- Attend mentor training.

- Willingness to communicate regularly with program staff, submit activity information and take constructive feedback.

- Have a clean criminal history.

- Not user of illicit drugs.

Desirable Qualities

- Willing listener.

- Encouraging and supportive.

- Patient and flexible.

- Tolerant and respectful of individual differences.

Benefits

- Personal fulfillment through contribution to community and individuals

- Satisfaction in helping someone mature, progress and achieve goals

Mentee Orientation Session

- Develop understanding of program.

- Mentee's roles and expectations.

- Begin to explore possible benefits of mentoring.

Mentor Screening Procedure

Mentoring staff should complete the steps below to determine if a candidate qualifies to become a mentor.

- Applicant must return all completed materials in application package.

- Mentor file should be created for all prospective mentors containing all information.

- The program staff should make an appointment and conduct an in-person interview with prospective mentor.

- Conduct phone interviews with personal references.

- Based on information gathered above, make an assessment and determine acceptance or rejection of prospective mentor.

- Send out letters of acceptance or rejection.

- If applicant is accepted, they must complete twenty-hours (20) training session.

Training Session

Once matched, each mentor must attend in-service training during the course of the year. Content for the in-service sessions will be determined based on feedback provided by mentors and mentees during the support meetings or based on the feedback and suggestions from mentors and mentees.

Failure to complete training sessions coupled with iden-tified match problems may result in the match being termi-nated and may result in exclusion from further involvement in the mentoring program.

The training workshops are geared to help new mentors:

- Develop a deeper understanding of mentor's roles and expectations.

- Learn strategies for effectively mentoring a youth.

- Understand clearly the program guidelines and policies.

Matching Procedure

To begin the matching process, the program management team will review the application package and determine match suitability between mentor and mentee. The greatest weight will be placed on the mentee preferences and needs. A match selection will be made using the match suitability criteria as a guide.

- Preferences of the mentor/mentee

- Similar gender/ethnicity

- Common interests

- Similar personalities

Once a match is made the prospective mentor will then be contacted and given information. The mentee will then be contacted and given the information of the mentor. The mentee is informed last to minimize disappointment if the mentor does not approve of the match. Once both parties tentatively agree to match, they will meet at the launch of the program. At this first meeting there should be an exchange of telephone numbers and addresses. Mentors will meet parents and can also exchange telephone numbers with them at the launch.

Match Support

- Once matched, the supervisory team will be assigned to support and monitor the mentor/ mentee relationship.

- Within one (1) month of the match, the supervising team will make contact with all parties to determine how meetings went.

- The assigned supervisor will then follow up monthly with each party to gather information regarding meeting dates, times, activities and how the match is proceeding.

If the supervisor assesses a potential problem with the match, they will attempt to clarify the potential problem and work with the mentor/mentee to resolve the issue early. At that time, it would be determined if either or both parties are suitable for re-matching with other partners

If the problem cannot be resolved, formally closing the match may be necessary. The process for resolving problems will follow the **IDEAL** model. This includes:

- **I**dentify the problem and have a clear shared understanding of the problem.

- **D**evelop alternative solutions that could address the problem.

- **E**valuate the strengths and weaknesses of each solution.

- **A**ct on the most constructive solution.

- **L**earn from how the solution worked and respect the **IDEAL** process if necessary.

- Every year **the Mentoring Program** will host a participant recognition event, or activity. A mentor and mentee award will be presented. An events planning committee will determine criteria for award and make final determination based on recommendations. Recognition will include a certificate and a nominal gift determined by the committee and budget allowance. Cards will also be sent to mentors during Christmas/New Year holiday and their birthday. All awards and recognitions will be featured in the **mentoring newsletter.**

Following are sample forms for the mentoring process

Mentor Acceptance Letter

Date

....

....

....

Dear ....

On behalf of the **Mentoring Program,** we are pleased to inform you of your acceptance as a mentor. Without eagerness of volunteers like you, we would be unable to accomplish our goal.

We thank you for taking the time and effort to join our program and we look forward to continuing to support you and assist you as a mentor.

At this time we are working on finding you a suitable match and will contact you as soon as possible.

Sincerely,

....

Parent/Guardian Referral Letter

To: _____

Your son/daughter has been referred to participate in the **Mentoring Program** that matches a community volunteer with a youth to serve as a one-on-one mentor.

The mentor would meet with your son/daughter once a week for a year and take personal interest in the growth and development of your son/daughter.

We hope that you will grant permission for your son/daughter to participate in the program.

 If you have any further questions please feel free to contact us.

I give informed consent for my son/daughter to participate in the mentoring program.

Signed:_____

Date :_____

Closure Letter

....

....

....

Dear...........................

This letter is to inform you that the mentoring relationship managed by the **Mentoring Program** has officially ended as of ....(date).

The Program no longer assumes responsibility for mentoring and supervising the match and your file will be on an inactive status. Future contact between match partners is at the sole discretion of all parties involved. Any incident occurring due to future contact among match participants is beyond the scope and responsibility of **Program.**

Thank you for your participation in the program. We look forward to your continued support.

Sincerely

....

INFORMATION RELEASE

I _____

understand that it will be necessary for the **Mentoring Program** to conduct a background check regarding criminal history, personal references and employment.

I hereby authorize the **Mentoring Program** to obtain any needed information regarding any history, character reference and employment for the purposes of participatory in a mentoring program.

_____

Signature

Mentor Contract

Name

Date

As a participant of the **Mentoring Program** I agree to:

Follow all the rules and guidelines as outlined by the program management, mentor training program policies and this contract.

Be flexible and provide the necessary support and advise to help my mentee succeed.

Make a one (1) year commitment to be a mentor.

Keep any information my mentee shares with me as confidential except as may cause him or others harm.

Attend in-service training sessions.

I agree to follow all the above stipulations of this program as well as any conditions as instructed by the program management.

_____ Date _____

Signature

Closure Procedure

The Program management team will follow the closure procedures as closely as possible. At the point it is decided that a match is closing, the supervisory team will instruct all participants through the closure process. All closures must be classified as to the reason for the match ending. The major classifications are as follows and the circumstances will dictate the procedure to be followed.

- Planned – A planned closure is one known about for a period of time. A common reason for planning a match closure may include end of program.

- Extenuating – Extenuating circumstances for match closure are usually more sudden in nature and beyond the control of the program.

- **Difficult** –A difficult match closure is due to relationships or behavioral difficulties i.e. lack of cooperation, irreconcilable issues, lack of compatibility, and/or violations of program policies.

In all cases, attempts will be made to have a closure meeting to include program staff, mentor, and mentee. The parent / guardian may attend if desired. The agenda should include, depending on circumstances of closure:

- Open discussion about relationship ending.

- Distribution of participant Closure Letter.

In all circumstances the parties should receive a Closure Letter stipulating the match has formally ended.

Where necessary the mentee will be counseled before being re-matched.

Marketing Strategy

Recruitment Plan

To attract one hundred (100) new mentors a year.

Target Audience

Men and women who reside within the country

Communication Message

Youths need role models, not critics. Be a mentor!

Promotional Materials

- Tri fold – Brochure
- Information flyers
- Newsletter
- Generic news article for newspaper
- Program presentation

Promotional Activities

- Place brochures and flyers throughout community.
- Display tables at various events.
- Distribution of quarterly magazine
- Presentation to community organizations and businesses.

Inquiry Procedure

All persons inquiring to be mentors must speak directly to program staff.

Program staff must follow the inquiry procedure as outlined below.

- All prospective mentor inquiries will be recorded by program staff.

- Program staff will give a brief verbal overview of program.

- Information Brochure will be given to persons who show interest in becoming a mentor.

- The Brochure will include information such as;

- Overview and purpose of program.

- Time and duration commitment

- Overview of screening requirements.

- Training requirements.

- Prospective participants will receive an application package.

Mentor Orientation Session

Objectives of Session:

- Generate enthusiasm among prospective.

- Provide a basic understanding of program and mentor roles and expectations.

- Explore simple and effective approaches to mentoring.

The Mentoring Process

Stages of the Program

- Pre-Planning

- Recruitment

- Orientation

- Induction and Training

- Matching

- Mentoring

- Termination

1. Pre Planning Stage

- Recruit a staff that will be committed to implement and monitor the program.

- Identify "At Risk" students; i.e, children who are prone to become involved in crime, drug use, school absenteeism or any other delinquent behavior.

- Obtain permission from parent/guardian for student to participate in program.

2. Recruitment

- Recruitment of mentor should be based on person's morals and values, ability to serve and ability to lead. Recruitment should be conducted after screening process.

- Identify adults who can act as a role model to youths

- Recruitment of youths should be based on their willingness to be part of the program and parental consent.

- Preference should be given to students of single parent home with little or no supervision.

3. Induction and Training

Identify skills needed for mentors; such as,

- Objective

- Open-minded

- Listening skills

- Optimistic

- Leadership

- Enthusiastic

- Adaptable

- Motivator

- Confidentiality

- Competent

- Teacher

- Role Model

- Expose mentors to their responsibility as a Mentor.

To ensure a productive relationship the mentor must take certain actions. These include:

- Set realistic expectations for mentee achievement and for their own involvement.

- Maintain consistent contact with mentee to help build relationship.

- Listen with empathy and provide emotional support.

- Give and receive constructive feedback.

- Expose mentee to existing opportunities.

- Guide mentee in exploring options.

Explain to mentors the objective of the program:

- To prevent permanent exclusion, truancy and school dropout.

- To encourage individuals to take responsibility for their thoughts, feelings, perception and behaviors.

- To teach individuals new and more positive ways of relating to their peers.

- To provide a support system for 'at risk' youths.

- To enable youths to strengthen their leadership and management skills and widen their career opportunities.

Training of Mentee

Mentee must be coached on their responsibility. These include the following.

- To set realistic goals with their mentor

- Communicate their problems clearly

- Be clear and open on his/her needs.

- Be open to feedback and accept information from mentor without interpreting it as evaluation.

- Practice self empowering behavior

- Initiate reasonable and frequent contact with the mentor.

- Recognize that mutual respect, trust and openness are the foundation for achieving mutual commitment to mutual goals.

- Contribute ideas about opinion for solving a given problem.

- Be responsible in keeping appointments with mentor.

4. Matching

Matching should be done based on similarities of mentors and mentees. These can be:

- Shared background

- Similar Interest

- Gender

- Ethnicity

- Career Aspirations

- Other logistical issues that would facilitate regular meetings.

5. Implementation

- Formal launching of the program

- Introduction of mentors to mentees and parents

- Formal period of program must be established

6. Monitoring

Establish monthly meetings with mentor and mentee to determine problems such as mismatch lack of communication or any other problem.

7. Evaluation

Based on objectives of program, identify evaluative tools for determining success or failure of program

The Mentoring Process

Stage I – Initiation

Mentor establishes rapport with mentee. This can begin in the first meeting, which should be the launching of the program.

Task involved

- Mentor and mentee exchange views on the type of relationship.

- Establish a formal contract

- Set conditions for working together, these will include days and time for meetings.

Dynamics

- There may be impatience to get going

- Politeness

- Testing out each other

- Challenges

Stage 2 – Getting Established

Task

- Identify mentee style of learning
- Determine mentee goals
- Set objective measures
- Identify priority areas for work
- Clarify focus of work
- Begin work

Dynamics

- Mentee may be unwilling to set goals
- Issues of trust may be evident

Skills needed

- Set up with mentee opportunities for diagnosing situations
- Give feedback
- Set objectives
- Provide guidance on each step

Stage 3--Developmental Phase

Task

- Create forum for processing mentee issues
- *Establish strategies for reviewing progress*
- Be ready for evolution of relationship

Dynamics

- A period of sustained productive activity

- Dealing with change in the relationship

- Preparing for transition

Skills needed

- *Monitor progress of mentee*

- Recognize achievement

- Manage evolution of relationship

Stage 4 – Termination

Task

- Allow relationship to end or evolve

- Move to maintenance of relationship

- Review what skills can be taken and used in other context

Dynamics

- Dealing with loss of the relationship

- Evaluation

Skills needed

- Address the feelings of loss

- Orchestrate good ending

- Establish friendship

MENTOR RECORD SHEET

Contact Date	Meeting Dates	Activities	Comments

Program Methodology

The program will use a participatory and collaborative approach as the major vehicle of delivery. This method affords other organizations greater opportunities to become involved in the mentoring process. It also allows mentees (At Risk youths) to participate in the decision making in respect to the activities in which both themselves and their mentors will engage.

A supervisory committee would be responsible for monitoring the relationship between mentor and mentee. A non-judgmental, confidential environment would be created during the mentoring process as a means of fostering trust, and deepening the mentoring relationship, thereby allowing mentees to comfortably share their experiences.

The program will include a training component targeting mentors in order to raise their awareness of youth related issues and maintain an ongoing discussion about changing needs and dynamics affecting the mentees. In this regard the focus will be on sharing knowledge and skills among the mentor group.

The strength of a mentoring program begins with agency support, resources and infrastructure. Research has indicated that the mentoring is most effective when the relationship last over a sustained period of time. It is therefore critical that the capacity exists to sustain program efforts for long term. This capacity can be reflected by policies, staffing, commitment and resources. In the absence of capacity, mentoring efforts will be at higher risk for failure.

Phase One

Program Design and Planning

The heart and soul of any mentoring program is found in its program design

The design will address the structure and format the program takes. This includes:

- Establishing of policies and procedures

- Implementation of ongoing training and professional development

- Developing a program budget

- Selection of a management team

- Establishing of case management protocol

- Designing of instruments for the monitoring and evaluation process

- Designing of instruments for screening and matching mentors.

- Designing a mentoring operational manual

- Determining objectives and outcomes

- Defining nature of mentoring sessions (support, socialization, career)

- Developing roles and responsibility chart

Phase Two

Screening Process & Orientation

- All applicants are required to complete this training process

- Screening sets the standards of eligibility for the program.

- Four (4) basic elements will be used for screening mentors:

1. Written Application

- This includes choice of days and times for meeting and preferred age of person they wish to work with.

- Application will include statement of applicant expectation and Special interest, which is helpful in matching Employment status.

2. Personal Interview

Discussion will include questions that will provide information about:

- Family relationship & History

- Interest & leisure time activities

- Attitudes & beliefs

- Use of alcohol & drugs

- Ability to sustain relationship

- Education

3. Character Reference Check (employment record)

4. Criminal background check

*Applicants must sign release agreement
to have these checks done.*

Orientation

Orientation clarifies roles, responsibility and expectations. This will include:

- Provide program overview

- Level of commitment expected

- Description of eligibility, screening process and suitable requirements

- Summary of program policies.

Phase Three

Training

The program structure is designed to expose mentors to specific skills and training through twenty contact hours of training in the first phase of the program. However training will be on going. The opportunity for skills building is provided through role play and simulated sessions conducted by qualified facilitators. Mentees training is typically shorter than mentors' as it mainly focuses on procedures and process of building stable relationship with an adult.

Phase Four

Program Management

Develop a comprehensive system for managing program information. A management information system will be developed to easily track the success and constraints in the program. This system will afford management the opportunity to easily:

- Maintain personal records

- Track program activity

- Document mentor/mentee matches

- Manage risk (i.e. relationship issues between mentor/mentee)

- Document program efforts

Design System to Monitor Program

The monitoring of the program is important to identify risk, mismatch and successes. The monitoring will include the following procedures.

- Review policies, procedures and operations on a regular basis

- Collect program information from staff, mentors and mentees

Develop a Social Marketing and Public Relations Plan

The intent of this plan would be to mobilize the support of all stakeholders and to ensure they are willing to participate in the program. These activities will include;

- Developing a marketing plan

- Identify target markets

- Developing partnership and collaboration with other organizations

- Holding recognition events for mentors/mentees and sponsors

Phase Five

Monitoring and Evaluation

It is important to find out if match is meeting and_ program rules followed. Monitoring can also track mentees functions in areas such as literacy levels, and general mood. Monitoring process includes defining the rules for problem solving, early termination as well as re matching.

Support and Retention Component

- Ongoing peer support groups will be established for mentors

- Ongoing training

- Relevant issue discussion and information dissemination

- Annual recognition and appreciation event

- Networking with appropriate organization

The evaluation component will be based on both impact and outcome analysis of the program. To ensure program quality and effectiveness the evaluation process will be as follows:

Develop a plan to measure program process

- Select indicators of program implementation viability, training hours and relationship duration.

- Develop system for collecting and managing specified data.

Develop a plan to measure program outcomes

- Select appropriate instruments to measure outcomes, such as questionnaire, focus groups and interviews

- Select and implement an evaluation design.

Create a process to reflect on and disseminate evaluation findings

- Refine the program design and operations based on findings

- Develop and deliver reports on a quarterly basis

CHAPTER TEN

Initiating a Mentoring Program

Why Implement Mentoring Programs

Many organizations and government entities are creating formal mentoring programs to deal with at-risk youth and indirectly to deal with dysfunctional families, crime and drug based community problems, personal academic failure, and generally antisocial and criminal activity among the young. Mentoring can become both a program for personal correction and a means of preventing a more drastic deterioration of the community environment. This becomes a benefit not only to the clients of the mentoring services, but the larger community can see positive change and consequently become more supportive of the formal mentoring process.

Formal Mentoring Programs

Formal mentoring programs are structured, have oversight, and have clear and specific organizational goals. Informal mentoring, on the other hand, has minimal to no structure or supervision and may not have a clear goal. Informal mentoring is normally for interpersonal enhancement, but can also promote growth and development of the young; however, an informal process does little to assist at-risk youth. However, the effectiveness of mentoring is dependent on clearly defined roles and expectations and a clear awareness of the benefits of participating in the mentoring process by all concerned. The author of this text firmly supports a formal and structured process with sufficient involvement to be effective.

A Face-to-face Session

Mentorship refers to a face-to-face relationship in which a more experienced mentor assists a less experienced mentee in dealing with both positive and negative aspects of their life and future.   Mentoring is a process that involves two-way communications and is relationship-based and usually uses both the formal or informal transmission of information relevant to the mentee and delivered in a face-to-face session for a sustained period. It is the personal interaction that is the key to effectiveness in the mentoring process.

Below are a dozen effective practices in implementing a program:

- Plan a strategy to deal with at-risk youth

- Match mentors and mentees

- Develop and conduct a program orientation

- Write guidelines for mentors, mentees, and managers.

- Prepare a contract for both mentor and mentee to sign

- Conduct a trial run to discover and solve problems

- Develop an plan of action based on goals

- Provide issues to discuss with mentees

- Provide session procedures

- Establish a separation process or terminal practice

- Arrange to recognize and reward finishers

- Evaluate periodically all mentoring outcomes

Some Programs Fail

Some mentoring programs fail for a variety of reasons. A few know reasons for failure are; (1) a lack of participation, (2) poor leadership, (3) inadequate advance planning, (4) idealistic expectations, (5) unclear goals, (6) limited follow-up, and (7) insufficient and limited evaluation together with feed-back for change. No program is perfect and constant upgrading and positive change is required to assure an on- going and effective program.

A Mentoring Program is a Partnership

Endeavors to mentor at-risk youth become a partnership between mentor and mentee, and among management, staff, and support partners. It is this common interaction that makes the enterprise work effectively. Mentoring has been identified as an important influence in positive change for at-risk youth. A major function of coaching and mentoring is to advance the personal development of at-risk youth and facilitate the use of practical problem-solving skills to create a more positive and personal involvement in the community. While such programs and relationships can produce positive results, the goal must be to develop an individual mentee to the point they can function personally and socially in their daily lives. Care must be taken that an at-risk youth does not develop a growing dependency on a mentor or the program. If clients do not learn to stand on their own two feet, the program fails. The best practice for longevity of an operation is when the community and partners can see positive results and crucial changes in the clients. Mentors nor financial supporters will not maintain involvement unless they witness positive change in clients and see a wise use of time and funds.

Benefits of Mentoring

As a result of being a mentor, an individual may develop an enhanced sense of personal and professional performance. To enjoy an enthusiasm for being a good role model is a direct benefit of mentoring at-risk youth. The pride of surrogate "parenting" brings out both the maternal and paternal traits of an individual mentor. The nature of this fulfillment of personal achievement cannot be purchased with money. A course of action that involves assisting at-risk youth generates an awareness of the real needs of the younger generation. The process of dealing with at-risk young people produces an understanding of the needs for a two-parent family in nurturing children. Involvement in mentoring enhances the skills of coaching, listening, counseling, and role modeling. The practice of personal leadership opens opportunities to share expertise and knowledge with the next generation.

Initiating a Mentoring Program

Those interested in initiating a mentoring program and desire consultation, may contact the author for guidance, materials, or to schedule a conference, workshop, or policy consultation via Email: ***ConsultOnYouth@gmail.com***

ABOUT THE AUTHOR

Joanne Spence is a motivational coach, lecturer, and behavior change therapist with a compelling interest in mentoring young people in difficult situations. She received a Bachelor's degree in Social Work with a minor in Management Information Systems and a Masters degree in Mediation with concentration on youth development from the University of the West Indies, St Augustine, Trinidad. Joanne earned a Doctor of Philosophy in areas of youth development from Oxford Graduate School (USA).

Dr. Spence is the chief consultant at a consulting firm in Trinidad and provides services in counseling, mediation and conflict resolution. She is also founder and director of **The Mentoring Centre of Trinidad and Tobago.** Author of three books, she has also written articles for several journals and magazines on topics such as youth crime and delinquency, and conflict resolution as well as having presented academic papers on crime and delinquency both at local and international forums. Joanne is the mother of three. Her career and professional objective is to develop a working model for a National Mentorship Program in Trinidad and Tobago that could be replicated in other countries with similar needs.

APPENDIX

References And Selected Reading

It should be noted that there appears to be a scarcity of
material between 2004 and 2011 on the subjects covered
in this book.

Allender, Dan B. (2006) *Leading with a Limp: Turning Your Struggles into Strengths*. Colorado Springs, CO: WaterBrook Press.

Barker, Gary. 2005. *Dying to be Men.* Youth Masculinity and Social Exclusion, London: Routledge.

Barrow, Christine. 1996. *Family in the Caribbean.* Themes and Perspective, Kingston, Jamaica: Weiner Publishers.

Barrow, Christine. 2001. *Children's Rights.* Caribbean Realities. Kingston: Ian Ramble Publishers.

Bowlby, John. 1961. *Process of Mourning.* International Journal of Psychoanalysis, 42, 317-340.

British Association of Social Workers. 1989. *Guide to Policy and Practice in the Management of Child Abuse:* Project Group Report, West Midlands: Wollaston Printing Services.

Bronfenbrenner, Urie. 1979. *The Ecology of Human Development.* Cambridge, MA: Harvard University Press.

Crawford-Brown, Claudia. 1999. *Who will save our children?* The plight of the Jamaican child in the 1990's? Mona Jamaica: Canoe Press.

Danns, George et al. 1997. *Tomorrow Adults.* A Situational Analysis of Youth in the Caribbean, Gender and Youth Affairs Division, London: Commonwealth Secretariat.

Deosaran, Ramesh. 2006. *Project Headway, African Youths in Danger on the East-West Corridor.* Research Policy Project in collaboration with Public Services Association, Trinidad: University of the West Indies, Centre for Criminology and Criminal Justice.

Deosaran, Ramesh. 2007. *Crime, Delinquency and Justice.* A Caribbean Reader, Kingston Jamaica: Ian Randle Publishers.

Deutsch, Morton. 1973. *The Resolution of Conflict.* Constructive and Destructive Processes, New Haven: Yale University Press.

Downes, Andrew. 1999. *Poverty and labour market status in the Caribbean.* Institute of Social & Economic Research. U.W.I. Cave Hill, Barbados: Caribbean Development Bank.

Flyvberg, Bent. 2006. *Five Misunderstandings about Case Study.* Research Qualitative Inquiry, 12.no. 2 April, 2004.

Furnham, Adrian. 1986. Culture Shock. Psychological Reactions to Unfamiliar Environment. Ed, Walter Lonner. London; Methuen.

Green, Hollis L. 2009. Remedial and Surrogate Parenting in the Custodial Arena., Nashville: GlobalEdAdvance Press.

Haralambos Michael, Martin Holborn. 2004. *Sociology Themes and Perspectives.* London: Harper Collins Publishers.

Health Economic Unit. 2005. *A Situational Analysis of Children Orphaned And Vulnerable To HIV- AIDS.* Trinidad: University of the West Indies, St Augustine.

Holder Dolly Jennifer, Sogren Michele. 2004. *The Impact of Domestic Violence on Children in Trinidad and Tobago.* Caribbean Journal of Social Workers,Vol 3:7-23 Arawak Publications.

Isenhart Myra, and Spangle Michael. 2000. *Collaborative Approaches to Resolving Conflict.* Thousand Oaks, California: Sage Publications.

Jones Adele, Jacqueline Sharpe, and Michele Sogren. 2001. *Children's Experiences Of separation from Parents as a consequence to Migration. Caribbean Journal of Social Workers.* Vol 3: 89-108, Jamaica: Arawak Publications.

Jones Adele, Padmore Jacqueline. 2004. *The Social Work Implication of HIV/ AIDS.* In The National Human Development Report, Trinidad: UNDP Report.

Krippendorff, Klaus. 1980. *Content Analysis. An introduction to its Methodology,* Beverly Hills: Sage Publication Ltd.

Krux, Edwards. 2000. *Mediation and Conflict Resolution in Social Work and Human Resources.* Chicago: Nelson Hall Publishers.

Lowicki J, Pillsbury. 2000. *Untapped Potential. Adolescents Affected by Armed Conflict, A Review of Programs and Policies,* New York: Women's Commission for Refuge Women and Children.

Marshall, Ronald. 2003. *Return to Innocence. A Study of Street Children in the Caribbean,* Theory, Research, and Analysis, Trinidad: University of the West Indies: School of Continuing Studies.

National Report on Development of Education in Trinidad and Tobago. 2004. *Quality Education for all young people.* Challenges, Trends, Priorities, Port of Spain: Ministry of Education.

Neubeck Kenneth, and Glasberg Devita. 2005. *Sociology.* Diversity, Conflict and Change, Boston: MacGraw Hill.

Newman, Jesse. 2005. *Protection through Participation.* Young People Affected by Forced Migration and Political Crisis, London: Refuge Study Centre, University of Oxford.

Office of Conflict Management and Mitigation, 2005. *Youth and Conflict.* A Tool for Intervention, Washington, DC: Office of Conflict Management and Mitigation, US AIDS.

Payne, Malcolm. 1997. *Modern Social Work Theory.* Chicago: Ylueum Books.

Roberts, Andy *(1999)* "The origins of the term mentor", *History of Education Society Bulletin, no 64, Nov 1999, p313-329.*

Roberts, Andy *(1999)* "The origins of the term mentor", *History of Education Society Bulletin, no 64, Nov 1999, p313-329.*

Rodgers, D. (1999). *Youth Gangs and Violence in Latin America and the Caribbean.* A Literature Survey Urban Peace Program Series, Washington, DC: The World Bank.

Shark, Jerry. *How to develop an operational manual for mentoring programs.*

Sharpe Jacqueline, Joan Bishop. 1993. *A Situational Analysis of Children in Especially Difficult Circumstances in Trinidad and Tobago.* Barbados: St. Michael. UNICEF,

Spence- Baptiste, Joanne (2004) Mentoring, A community Approach. *Trinidad: Blessed Digital Services*

Trinidad and Tobago Youth and Social Development: An Integrated Approach for Social Inclusion *(2000) Adapted from the Vanier Institute's definition*

Trinidad and Tobago, Central Statistical Data. 2007 Population Census. Port of Spain: Central Statistical Office.

Trinidad and Tobago, Ministry of Youth, Sports, Culture and Creative Arts. 1991. *Survey of Youth Problems and Perceptions.* Port of Spain: Ministry of Youth Sports, Culture and Creative Arts.

Trinidad and Tobago, National Youth Policy Task Force. 2005. *National Youth Policy.*Port of Spain, Trinidad: The Government Printery.

Trinidad and Tobago, Youth Social Development. 2000. *Summary Data on General Economic Situation of Trinidad and Tobago.* Port of Span: Central Statistical Office.

Trinidad and Tobago. 1994. Ministry of Education, Education Policy Paper (1993-2003) *National Task Force Report on Education.* White Paper. Trinidad and Tobago: Ministry of Education.

United Nations Children Educational Fund. 2002. *Report on Multiple Indicators of HIV/AIDS.* National Human Development Report, Research Paper.

Varma, Ved. 1997. *Troubles of Children and Adolescents.* London: Jessica Kingsley Publishers.

World Health Organization. 2002. *World Report on Violence and Health.* Geneva: World Health Organization.

CPSIA information can be obtained at www.ICGtesting.com
Printed in the USA
LVOW01s2304110714

394045LV00010B/100/P